I'd Rather Be Dead
Than Be a Girl

Implications of Whitehead, Whorf, and Piaget
for Inclusive Language in Religious Education

John Marcus Sweeney

Julie,
Thank you for your
involvement in RUCC,
and this class.
All my best wishes!
John

John M. Sweeney

University Press of America,® Inc.
Lanham · Boulder · New York · Toronto · Plymouth, UK

Copyright © 2009 by
University Press of America,® Inc.
4501 Forbes Boulevard
Suite 200
Lanham, Maryland 20706
UPA Acquisitions Department (301) 459-3366

Estover Road
Plymouth PL6 7PY
United Kingdom

Library of Congress Control Number: 2009934251
ISBN-13: 978-0-7618-4872-1 (clothbound : alk. paper)
ISBN-10: 0-7618-4872-X (clothbound : alk. paper)
ISBN-13: 978-0-7618-4873-8 (paperback : alk. paper)
ISBN-10: 0-7618-4873-8 (paperback : alk. paper)
eISBN-13: 978-0-7618-4874-5
eISBN-10: 0-7618-4874-6

Dedication

From the past for all of their support and their examples

Ruth
Beverley

Into the present for their encouragement and love

Sharon
William
Charles
Mary
Scott

Towards the future

Samantha Hope, Owen Frederick, and Elliott Bradley
may their world become more just

Copyright Permissions

Contents

Preface

I have been interested in "life, the universe, and everything" (with apologies to Douglas Adams, *Hitchhiker's Guide to the Galaxy*) for almost 40 years now, this interest beginning in my undergraduate days. During my senior year in college, I encountered the writings of Alfred North Whitehead, a philosopher truly interested in "life, the universe, and everything." Whitehead had begun the process (no pun intended) of developing a metaphysics for all occasions (pun intended), a truly descriptive cosmological story. More amazing was Whitehead's insistence that all the evidence be considered, that the system be changed as needed in the quest for metaphysical explanation, and that participation in the ongoing struggle to deal with "life, the universe, and everything" is a worthwhile endeavor. Even those philosophers and philosophical systems at odds with Whiteheadian thought should be explainable by, or within, a philosophy of organism.

Whitehead did not try to protect his proposals from alteration. Rather, Whitehead encouraged expansion of the system and exploration of the various possibilities as they occur. Even mistakes and disagreements need to be accounted for in a truly metaphysical system, and changes in this system are encouraged. For example, there are Whiteheadian theodicies and "classical" theodicies; in a descriptive cosmology, as the philosophy of organism hopes to be, both kinds of theodicies, as well as the discrepancies between the two approaches, should be explainable.

The Whiteheadian approach stands in stark contrast to the vast majority of the other thinkers and systems that I have studied. These thinkers and systems, especially but not only in the Anglo-American analytic philosophical tradition, prefer to explain away data that does not fit into their system (such as the placebo effect), or to caricature and then dismiss that which was misrepresented (as I have heard done regarding the Sapir-Whorf Hypothesis), or to ignore information they consider to be trivial (such as evidence regarding paranormal experience).

Another unacknowledged difficulty many thinkers regularly encounter involves their willingness to make exceptions or to otherwise build in special cases, after they have said "no exceptions" or "no special cases." For example, Jean Calvin claimed he was going to be thoroughly logical, yet most of the time when he got himself into a logical corner he claimed the solution was to be found in the "mystery of God." Both Sigmund Freud and B. F. Skinner have written as if human freedom were a real possibility, but in following their assumptions and views, one will find that freedom will need to be some sort of very special case; freedom is not inherent in either system. A Whiteheadian approach suggests that freedom, not just human freedom, is part of the cosmic process from the very beginning and is present in the very foundations of the process. Accordingly, neither a special case nor an exception to the metaphysical rules is needed.

Since I began studying philosophy, theology, psychology, and education, I have consistently found process thought in general, and Whitehead's philosophy of organism in particular, to be the best approach to use in attempting to explain "life, the universe, and everything."

This study, then, is greatly influenced both by the philosophy of organism proposed Alfred North Whitehead and by the spirit towards philosophical investigation that is expressed in Whiteheadian thought. By the "spirit" of Whitehead's philosophy, I mean primarily the attitude towards speculative philosophy. Since Whitehead's philosophy of organism serves as the background for all the chapters in this study, presenting more information on the spirit of this philosophy is appropriate.

"Speculative Philosophy is the endeavour to frame a coherent, logical, necessary system of general ideas in terms of which every element of our experience can be interpreted" (Whitehead, 1978, p. 3). For Whitehead, then, speculative philosophy is the attempt to provide a complete description of how this world functions, a description that in principle can be applied to all aspects of the universe.

> The true method of discovery is like the flight of an aeroplane. It starts from the ground of particular observation; it makes a flight in the thin air of imaginative generalization; and it again lands for renewed observation rendered acute by rational interpretation. (Whitehead, 1978, p. 5)

As this quotation suggests, speculative philosophy begins with "particular observation" which then serves as the basis for "imaginative generalization," that is, proposed explanations of that which has been observed. Discrepancies between explanation and initial observation lead to "renewed observation," renewed explanation, and so on. The philosophical process is on-going and open-ended; the probability is very small that all metaphysical principles will ever be known and thoroughly understood (Whitehead, 1978, p. 4).

The open-ended nature of speculative philosophy suggests that the metaphysical principles developed in the course of one's investigation need to be open to regular revision. A Whiteheadian approach to speculative philosophy encourages participants to take account of as much evidence as possible; evidence is not to be discounted merely because it does not easily fit with an accepted theory. For too many philosophers, "failure to include some obvious elements of experience in the scope of the system is met by boldly denying the facts" (Whitehead, 1978, p. 6). By contrast, if one encounters facts that do not fit with one's theory, the theory needs to be adjusted.

Since one of the goals of metaphysics or speculative philosophy, from a Whiteheadian perspective, is to provide description that covers as much of reality as possible, there should be no surprise in learning that Whiteheadian thought encourages such wide-ranging description. The metaphysical principles ought to be of such a nature that they can assist in the description of every event, circumstance, or situation that occurs. Metaphysical description involves all practice and all the facts; if there is a problem, alter the metaphysics, not the facts (Whitehead, 1978, p. 12).

> Being tackled at Rugby, there is the Real. Nobody who hasn't been knocked down has the slightest notion of what the Real is. . . . I used to play in the middle

of the scrum. They used to hack at your shins to make you surrender the ball, a compulsory element—but the question was how you took it—your own self-creation. Freedom lies in summoning up a mentality which transforms the situation, as against letting organic reactions take their course. (Hendley, 1986, p. 75; Whitehead quoted in William Ernest Hocking 'Whitehead as I Knew Him,' *Journal of Philosophy*, 14 September 1961:512.)

Whitehead encourages exploration and application of the philosophy of organism. As indicated above, when one discovers changes that need to be made, then one needs to make them. A truly speculative philosophy needs to be able to explain even the apparently most mundane aspects of reality. Metaphysical description that cannot adequately explain "the middle of the scrum" needs to be revised.

A frequent tendency against which Whitehead warns is what Whitehead calls "the fallacy of misplaced concreteness." As the label suggests, this fallacy occurs in mistaking an abstraction for the concrete reality to which the abstraction refers. Focusing on and labeling a pattern of events in nature may be useful for some purposes, but the actual events should not be equated with the pattern that has been abstracted from them. "This fallacy consists in neglecting the degree of abstraction involved when an actual entity is considered merely as far as it exemplifies certain categories of thought" (Whitehead, 1978, pp. 7-8). For example, when the stages proposed by a structural analysis are believed to exist independently of the actual phenomena to which the analysis refers, then the fallacy of misplaced concreteness has occurred. The stages are labels referring to patterns of behavior.

From a Whiteheadian perspective, an 'object' of sense-perception is an abstraction; that is, any object sensorily perceived is the result of a sophisticated process, at the base of which is primitive, concrete, particular experience. Sense-perception is the process by which very basic feelings and experiences are received and discriminated into sense-impressions (Olewiler, 1971, pp. 178-185). Assuming objects of sense-data to be ultimate reality would be committing the fallacy of misplaced concreteness.

Much of traditional Western philosophy has been predicated upon an "either-or-but-not-both" approach to problems and situations. That is, there has been a focus on simple, and usually false, oppositions, such as either God is completely transcendent or completely immanent, human beings are either completely free or completely determined. Whiteheadian thought suggests a more inclusive, a "both-and," approach to problems and situations, realizing that in daily life shades of gray and complexity are more frequent than oversimplified dichotomies. As indicated in this study, sexist language is a multilayered situation not easily correctable by doing simply either this or that. Both this and that will be needed.

In keeping with the spirit of Whiteheadian thought, this study explores a threefold thesis. This tripartite thesis is that language shapes how human beings perceive reality, that the development of theoretical constructs can help explain resistances to and possibilities for inclusive language, and that the implementation of inclusive language is an important goal for religious education. Chapter 1 provides some description of the role of sexist language in perpetuating sexual discrimination. Chapter 2 presents the thesis, discusses several notions of particular relevance to this work, introduces the three perspectives used in this study, and makes explicit some of the assumptions made in this study. Chapters 3, 4, and 5 present insights from the works of Alfred North Whitehead's philosophy of organism, Benjamin Lee Whorf's principle of linguistic relativity, and Jean Piaget's genetic epistemology that are especially relevant to this study. Chapter 6 summarizes the study up to this juncture and discusses the first two subtheses of the tripartite thesis. Chapter 7 discusses the third subthesis, the importance of inclusive language for religious education. Chapter 8 presents some strategies for implementing inclusive language, discusses some objections to inclusive language, and indicates how new self-critical linguistic habits can contribute to the advancement of humanity.

John M. Sweeney
Angelus Oaks, California

Chapter 1
Patriarchy and Sexist Language

Ask the boys and girls in your circle what they would like to be when they grow up. Then ask them what they would like to be if they were the opposite sex. (Smith, 1985b, p. 28)

If your findings correspond with mine you will discover more often than not: That when girls are asked what they would want to do if they were boys, they elevate the conventional prestige of their choice. So, for example, if as a girl they wanted to be nurses, as boys they might want to become doctors. Boys, on the other hand, often seem to find it impossible to think of themselves as girls and many answer simply, 'Nothing.' (Smith, 1985b, p. 29)

In a third grade class of a parochial school in Brooklyn, some 25 boys and girls were asked what they would like to be when they grew up. Then they were asked what they would like to be if they (were) the opposite sex. In many cases when the girls imagined themselves as boys, they raised the conventional prestige of their career choice. In too many cases the boys simply could not wrap their minds around the possibility of being a girl. One boy succinctly verbalized his non-plussed reaction, 'I'd kill myself!' (Smith, 1985a, p. 638)

In a philosophy class discussion on the topic of sexual equality, a woman related how disappointed her fifth-grade sister was to discover that she could not be a "fireman."[1]

Two three-year-old girls, one in California and one in New York, are being raised in a family where both parents work outside the home, share the housework, and are trying to be nonsexist in their language use. Each girl comes home from preschool and tells her parents that she wants to be a nurse. Asked why not a doctor, each girl insists that only men can be doctors.

"Kings are royaler than queens" a young girl tells her mother because on Mister Rogers "the King answers the questions the most" (Sheldon, 1990, p. 7).

As the preceding stories suggest, children (elementary school-age and younger) learn that being a boy or a man is "better than" being a girl or a woman, at least in English-speaking cultures, such as the United States of America. These stories are not unusual. In other words, the language and behavior of children indicate that sexism, that is, the various forms of harmful and unnecessary discrimination that occur against girls and women, is imparted to and implanted in children very early in life.

One of the ways this control shows and reinforces itself is in the language that people use. Consider the following studies:

---

1. This discussion occurred in the course "Introduction to Philosophy," Fall 1988, Mt. San Antonio College, Walnut, California.

> College students asked to select pictures to illustrate captions like 'Social Man' and 'Urban Man' were more likely to choose pictures of men only than pictures of men and women; with the 'generic' man removed from the legends ('Social Behavior,' 'Urban Life'), significantly fewer students selected pictures of men only. (Frank & Treichler, 1989, p. 8)

> Studies of grade school and junior high school students consistently reveal that students associated more men-only illustrations with the masculine 'generics' than with alternative forms. (Frank & Treichler, 1989, p. 8)

Others studies indicate the ways in which language influences human perception. For example, studies have indicated that students ranging from elementary school through high school and into college consistently believe job descriptions containing the so-called generic "he" or "man" to be intended for males (Frank & Treichler, 1989, p. 8). Also, studies have shown that when nonsexist pronouns are used in place of the so-called generic pronouns, "students make significantly fewer errors in comprehension" (Frank & Treichler, 1989, p. 8). Further, there is research that indicates that the words heard and images seen by children on television affect children's beliefs about the world. In particular, children who viewed shows with women portrayed as positive role models are more likely to develop positive attitudes about themselves and the role of women in society (Frank & Treichler, 1989, pp. 8-9).

Based upon the aforementioned studies and more, Frank and Treichler go on to state: "Taken as a whole, this body of research supports the hypothesis that linguistic usage shapes and reinforces selected cognitive tendencies, usually those in conformity with widely accepted cultural practices and beliefs" (Frank & Treichler, 1989, p. 9). Since current "cultural practices and beliefs" in the United States include biases against women, the English currently used in the United States likewise includes biases against women.

Learning sexism begins early in life, and language is one of the necessary means by which sexism is conveyed. Babies are treated differently depending upon whether they are perceived as boys or girls; even though baby "boys cry more and need less sleep than girls" (Wren, 1989, p. 28). Mothers attend to daughters more than sons. Both parents smile and talk to baby girls more than to baby boys (Wren, 1989, pp. 28-31). Further, baby girls and baby boys are talked to differently.

> A hail-baby-well-met style for little boys and a gentler dealing with little girls were owned by a group of parents who admitted calling their daughters Sweetie, Pudding, Doll-baby, Daddy's Pet, Daddy's Little Sweetheart, and boys Bronco, Cowboy, Polar Bear, Little Nut! (Morton, 1985, pp. 22-23)

Learning sexism also can be demonstrated in the way and by the words used by mothers as they talk about themselves to their children. Poynton (1989, pp. 25-26) discusses situations in which mothers underplay their own roles and contributions. For example, housework is rarely verbalized as tiring and important; mothers talk about "clever Daddy" and "silly mummy." "Mothers who pass on such 'knowledge' of female inferiority to their children have themselves internalised it from just such messages as they are now passing onto their children" (Poynton, 1989, p. 26). If it is true that "by the age of four children have a firm knowledge of sex identity and are well able to perceive distinctions of gender role" (Poynton, 1989, pp. 28-29), then sexist language and behavior would appear to be well on its way to a firm foundation in young children.

However, the process does not stop with young children. The training in sexism continues into formal schooling. Within the education system, boys are valued more highly than girls: boys talk more and require more attention than girls; the interests of boys are taken more seriously than the interests of girls; and autonomous behavior by boys is more rewarded than is such behavior by girls (Poynton, 1989, pp. 31-37). The boy is challenged to do better; the girl is told that "it (academic success) is beyond her," that this inability to succeed academically is natural, and that this inability is not her fault (Wren, 1989, pp. 28-31).

> In mixed-sex classes boys get more teacher time and are punished more for nonacademic faults whereas girls get less teacher time, are reprimanded more for academic mistakes, and are praised more for conduct and appearance than attainment. (Wren, 1989, p.28)

From infancy through the preschool years and into school age, "the everyday discourse with which children are surrounded from the day of their birth, in which they themselves become eventual participants, is a primary means by which socialisation is effected" (Poynton, 1989, p. 3). Since much of this discourse is sexist, it is not surprising that the socialization process itself tends to be sexist.

Patriarchy

Patriarchy is one way of describing the comprehensive system by which males maintain control and of which sexism is an aspect.

> By patriarchy I mean a culture that is slanted so that men are valued a lot and women are valued less; or in which men's prestige is up and women's prestige is down. (Gray, 1982, p. 19)

> Patriarchy may be defined as any social system in which men are perceived as inherently superior and more powerful than women. (Morton, 1985, p. 37)

In the United States of America, men and what men do are valued more than women and what women do. In the United States, a male high school dropout has the same earning potential as a female college graduate (Lazarus, 1987); white women who work full-time earn $.64 for each $1.00 that white men earn (Faludi, 1991, p. 364; National Public Radio). By 1988, black women were earning $.59 for each $1.00 that white men earned, and Hispanic women were earning $.54 for each $1.00 that white men earned (Faludi, 1991, p. 364). In

Chapter 13 of *Backlash*, Faludi (1987, pp. 363-399) demonstrates the increasing disparities in pay between women and men—that occupations in which women have traditionally been dominant are less well paying than occupations in which men dominate; that occupations in which men used to dominate but no longer do, relative wages have declined, such as insurance adjusters; and that in occupations wherein men and women have more or less equal access, the pay of men exceeds that of women for comparable work, as in public relations. The number of women in elected office, especially at the national level, remains far below the proportion of women in the population. Also, the portrayal of women in advertising, as presented in the film "Still Killing Us Softly" (Lazarus, 1987), is much more negative than the portrayal of men. Men are viewed as more important than women in the United States.

Within this patriarchal system a number of beliefs are promoted, and these beliefs in turn provide support for the patriarchy. Among these beliefs are the following:

> Reality is hierarchical and is supposed to be so—the justification can be either Divine or Nature. Power issues from the top, and those below are expected to obey. (Gray, 1982, p. 81)

> Man is special, unique and superior to all of Nature, and therefore can do what he wants—either due to Divine Fiat or by being the peak of evolution. (Gray, 1982, p. 86)

> Nature is feminine—a compliant woman with virgin resources to be used; a mother who will always protect you, giving you what you need and want; a wanton woman to be dominated. (Gray, 1982, p. 102)

> Subordinate groups are helpless and need to be taken care of by the powerful males; such care-taking legitimates the authority of those in control. (Russell, 1985, p. 596)

These and other related beliefs combine with behavior and lead to "the universal oppression of women, the poor, the nonwhite, the domination of Third World peoples, to world wars, and the exploitation of the earth and its resources" (Morton, 1985, p. 37). "The patriarchal mindset decides the truth and draws the line, and suddenly those outside that line become heretics" (Russell, 1985, p. 590). As historical evidence indicates, in the Salem Witch Trials for example, those considered heretics may be ignored, may be harassed, may be tortured, or may even be killed.

There are numerous, interrelated factors contributing to the continuing dominance of patriarchy: greed, apathy, fear, nationalism, covert operations, ego-centeredness, male control of social custom, male control of symbols and images—religious and mythic—to name but a few. Language plays one of the key roles in the continuing dominance of patriarchy, specifically through the contribution that sexist language makes by reinforcing the usually inferior, sometimes invisible, status of women and by influencing the development of children—both girls and boys.

Men have defined and controlled people's perceptions (Gray, 1982, p. 2). One of the means by which perceptions are defined and controlled is through the use of "so-called male generic language" (Gray, 1982, p. 71). Such language consists of claiming that the use of language such as "man," "mankind," "he," and "his," includes women as well as men in certain situations, for example "all men are created equal" or "if a policeman stops a person, then he should do what he says." So-called male generic language has become ingrained to such a degree that alternatives to such language are very difficult to consider; the habit is firmly entrenched.

> The difficulty is that if one has grown up surrounded by a particular set of 'messages,' or 'instructions' about how one should see, think, feel, act, and talk about the nature and purposes of social institutions in which one is involved, it is extremely difficult to even conceive of the possibility of there being a vantage point from which one might see things differently, much less to actually situate oneself at such a strategic place. (Poynton, 1989, pp. 12-13)

One of the more detrimental effects of the "so-called male generic language" is that it "serves to perpetuate the illusion that 'male' is synonymous with 'human'" (Gray, 1982, p. 71), thereby giving justification for ignoring women and any views that question the male perspective.

> Taking their cue from sexist language, women as well as men have assumed that all creatures are male unless there is prior evidence that they are female. Of course this assumption enhances male ego and virtually wipes out female presence, even to women themselves. (Withers, 1984, p. 14)

Sexist language contributes to the internalizing of sexist images, attitudes, and behaviors. Nelle Morton testifies to one outcome of this process: "The internalization of such male imagery prevented me from fighting for myself during my years at Drew University" (Morton, 1985, p. 192). And the mother cited earlier, whose child stated that "Kings are royaler than Queens," writes:

> What I see happening with my daughter is that this convention [pseudo-generic 'he'] in her language is causing her to think in a child's very concrete sense that more 'he's' than 'she's' actually exist out there in the world.
> Females become invisible if you rarely refer to them. (Sheldon, 1990, p. 5)

Another effect to which sexist language in general and so-called male generic language in particular contributes is a type of Catch-22. On the one hand, women who act "like men," that is, women who are brave, assertive, successful, and so on, tend to be viewed as deviant or unwomanly. On the other hand, women who act "like women," that is, women who are unstable, emotional, helpless and so on, tend to be discounted and devalued. Either way, women cannot win; if the male is identical with the human, then females cannot be success-ful.

Women also are slighted in study of the history of the English language as illustrated in *The Story of English*, a PBS series as well as a book by the same name. The title of the series suggests there is only one version of "the story" (Penelope, 1990, p. 26). Neither the series nor the book contains any references to feminist research on the English language. Additionally, neither the series nor the book discusses "the fact that Middle English speakers rejected the possibility of a sex-neutral pronoun in English" (Penelope, 1990, pp. 26-27). Finally, there is only one reference to male domination in the English language, a mention of the word "wimmin" in the Introduction (McCrum, Cran, & MacNeil, 1986, p. 15). Apparently *The Story of English* is yet another attempt, perhaps uncon-scious, to maintain male control of the English language.

> Patriarchy is at the root of the problem of inclusive language and power. Language both shapes and is shaped by the social world it names. In a patri-archal world of domination and subordination, language is a powerful tool for the exclusion of the weak. (Russell, 1985, p. 593)

Resistance to Change

There have been, and continues to be, a variety of responses to the claim that the English language as currently practiced is sexist and to the challenge to use the English language more inclusively. Responses to the claim that English is sexist and to the challenge to use more inclusive English range along a con-tinuum. At one end of the continuum, the claim is acknowledged and the chal-lenge accepted; at the other end of the continuum, both the claim and the chal-lenge are completely rejected. An important argument given by many who reject both the claim and the challenge is that language and thought are not connected in any way, or at least not in any significant way. Another argument used by many who reject both the claim and the challenge, yet who agree that society is sexist, is that there are other reasons for sexism, such as societal structures. Lan-guage, at best, is a minor concern that will become less sexist as the other fac-tors become less sexist. Yet, if language really is so trivial, then changing the language should be relatively easy; yet such change has not been easy. There has been, and continues to be, much resistance. Accordingly, the role language in the perpetuation of sexism is not as trivial as some have claimed.

> Male omnipresence in our vocabulary is only one of the ways in which women have been kept invisible in our society when they moved beyond traditional roles. If sexist terms are really so innocuous and trivial, why is everyone so anxious to protect them? (Nilsen, Bosmajin, Gershung, & Stanley, 1977, p. 74)

Even those who acknowledge the power of language to affect thought, percep-tion, and behavior have been resistant to changing sexist language.

Attempts to change sexist usage meet not merely with resistance, but with ridicule. It is odd that such ridicule often comes from the very people who profess their faith in the power of the words—linguists, literary critics, members of the MLA [Modern Language Association of America]. (Nilsen, Bosmajin, Gershung, & Stanley, 1977, p. 12)

Resistance to the use of truly inclusive language continues: (a) In the courses that I teach, sexist language is commonplace, and even feminists and language-sensitive males regularly "slip" into using sexist language, indicating that deeply ingrained linguistic habits are difficult to alter; (b) in churches, the struggle continues; sexist language is not being changed easily (Withers, 1984, pp. 13-16); Christian churches continue to use sexist language and promote sexist images—in hymns, in liturgies, in prayers, in meetings; (c) the mass media, especially television, continue to be sexist in both language and images—so much so that any use of "he or she" is startling. Overall, this resistance to inclusive language would appear to indicate both that society is patriarchal and that God is thought to be a male (Morton, 1985, pp. 20 & 150).

Concluding Remarks

One perspective of this study is that the relationship between language and thought is complex, involving perception, behavior, and other factors. All aspects of our life influence all the other aspects. Accordingly the language that is used influences thought, and vice versa; the degree of influence and interrelatedness with other factors is the topic under consideration in later chapters of this study.

As the stories and studies cited here indicate, young children have acquired the view that being a boy is better than being a girl. This perception is illustrated in their words as well as in their behavior. One purpose of this study is to investigate how such a perception is acquired, or ingrained, at such an early age. There are many factors that contribute to sexism; language is not the only source of sexism. Many factors are involved in socialization.

[I]t is important to be aware of the subtle learning that takes place because of (or through the power of) words in relation to other biases in our society including race, class, religion, age, and physical handicaps. (Withers, 1985, p. 510)

Language appears to be a necessary but not sufficient condition in the development and maintenance of sexist attitudes and behaviors.

Ours is also a racist society, an enthnocentric society, and an ecologically exploitative society, but neither time nor space permits discussion of these concerns and the role that language plays in their continuance; all of these "isms" (racism, sexism, ethnocentrism, and so on) are bound up with each other. This situation works towards the benefit of those in power. "Everything that happens to us we filter through the lens or screen of our understanding of the world" (Gray, 1982, p. 39). If our "lens" is patriarchal, then we will accept the patriarchal view of life, without much fuss as many, perhaps most, of us do. In addition to sexism the current patriarchal lens includes, as suggested above, racism, ethnocentrism, and more. To change this "lens" takes effort since trying to change deeply-ingrained habits can be quite difficult. Yet language can be one of the tools used to overthrow these same elites. Increasing sensitivity to linguistic issues, especially in the use of inclusive language, is one way of dealing with this situation for those who wish to effect some change in themselves as well as in others. In other words, while sexist linguistic habits are one of the ways of maintaining the status quo, changing these linguistic habits and implementing a truly inclusive language would be one factor in moving the status quo towards more inclusiveness.[2]

---

2.   For those who doubt the power of language, Wren (1989, pp. 15-16) cites the role of language in Nazi propaganda, especially as that language was used against the Jews, people who were regularly called a "plague" and "bacillus" who eventually "had" to be "exterminated."

Chapter 2
Thesis, Notions, and Perspectives

The threefold thesis of this study is that language shapes how human beings perceive reality, that the development of theoretical constructs can help explain resistances to and possibilities for inclusive language, and that the implementation of inclusive language is an important goal for religious education. Beginning in infancy, children are immersed in taken-for-granted linguistic structures and habits. These structures and habits strongly influence, sometimes to the point of virtually determining, the human perception of reality as well as the development of human attitudes and behaviors. Further, in English-speaking culture these linguistic habits have been, and still tend to be, sexist and exclusive; such linguistic habits form one of the supports for patriarchy as described in Chapter 1. The basis for a more inclusive language can be provided, and the implementation of this new approach would contribute significantly to changing persons and changing society.

This view of "change the language, change the person," occurs in popular culture, as demonstrated in the musical *My Fair Lady*, especially in the song entitled "Why Can't the English Learn to Speak?" If one of the goals of religious education is to promote the development of new persons, thereby contributing to the transforming of society, then the use of truly inclusive language throughout the life and work of religious institutions becomes one way of effecting such development.

To say that the English language helps to promote sexism is not the same as saying that every use of the language is sexist or that each and every person who uses the language is always sexist. The initial claim is inductive: Most of us, most of the time, especially when we are not paying attention or if we are not developing inclusive language habits, use the English language in sexist ways. The English language is flexible enough so that the sexist tendencies can be overcome if the speaker is aware, encouraged, and works on developing inclusive language habits. Overcoming the sexist tradition in English language usage is possible, either by conscious effort (which includes bringing sexist thoughts, attitudes, and images from unconsciousness into consciousness) or by early training and exposure (although until the mass media changes, the most that this approach may be able to do is plant some inclusive seeds) or some combination of the two. Motivations may emerge from personal experiences of sexism or other types of exclusion that can then be related to sexism. For example, males who feel excluded or oppressed may be more easily led to "see" and to "feel" a little of the oppression felt by women.

The focus of this dissertation is on American English as written and spoken in the mass media, in schools of various levels and kinds, and in other everyday usage, and as codified in standard dictionaries. The interplay between subcultures and dialects of English, such as Gullah and surf-speak, is beyond the scope of this study. However, most if not all variations of English are likely to be sexist, especially when used in unthoughtful ways. Claims regarding non-English languages are not pursued in this study, although there is evidence that Chinese and Japanese, for instance, are also sexist (Holgerson as cited in Regan,1989, pp. 28-30; Penelope, 1990, pp. 79-88).

Important Notions

Several of the more significant ideas for this study are (a) "language" and "inclusive language," (b) "education" and "religious education," (c) "theoretical constructs," (d) "perception," and (e) "transformation." Discussion of these terms follows.

Language and Inclusive Language

In this study, language refers to a complex of descriptions involving the words themselves, the meaning associated with the words, the patterns in which the words are or can be found, the meanings associated with those patterns, and the uses to which words, meanings, and patterns are put.

> [H]uman language is . . . accurately understood as the signs, sounds, gestures, marks, and expressions used to communicate ideas and feelings. Such communication is an essential part of human nature and provides the means of establishing relationships with others and discovering personal identity in communal relationships. (Russell, 1985, p. 585)

Language involves words and the systems of rules that are useful for speakers saying what they want to say (Penelope, 1990, p. xiii).

Language is a word with much potential ambiguity or vagueness attending closely to it. Further, language is a word with which many other concepts associate, concepts such as indexical, lexical, semantics, syntactic, grammatical, speech, and writing. Semantics and grammar are two of the more frequently used terms with the most comprehensive descriptions, with semantics referring to the various forms of meaning involved with linguistic usage and grammar referring to the various structures involved in language. Language can also be viewed as "a purely human and non-instinctive method of communicating ideas, emotions, and desires by means of a system of voluntarily produced symbols" (Sapir, 1949, p. 8). Alternatively, language can be viewed as involving (a) phonology, that is, the sound system, (b) morphology, that is, the construction of words based upon morphemes, (c) syntax, that is, the internal structure of sentences, and (d) semantics, that is, the abstract features of vocabulary, with all four levels working simultaneously and interacting with each other (Penelope, 1990, p. 239).

There are at least three factors involved in language usage: (a) the intent or purpose of the user, (b) the context in which and the audience for which the words are being used, and (c) the awareness of both users and receivers of each other and of the context. Generally, the intention(s) of the user and the context in which language is being used are relevant to the style of language actually used. For example, a person may want to express sexist views overtly and thus use language that clearly indicates the subordinate position that women are to occupy. In another situation, a focus on freedom may subtly limit the consideration of how language functions; "freedom for all men" may indeed be intended to mean "freedom for all people," and the context may help convey that particular intention.

There also may be situations in which the language is used, either unintentionally or intentionally, to mask an ugly reality; for example, the term pedophilia veils the fact that children have been sexually victimized by adults. There may be situations in which subversive or shocking language is needed or desired for the purpose of getting an audience's attention; perhaps one refers to God as "She" in order to get the crowd thinking about their unconscious assumptions regarding Divine sexuality. Also, there may be linguistic usages that have one meaning in one context and a different meaning in a different context—for example, the various ways in which the hymn "Amazing Grace" is used and interpreted. Whether linguistic usage is neutral or subversive or accurate or some combination thereof largely depends upon the context in which that language is being used and upon the intention with which the language is being used.

Another meaningful difference to note is the one between nonsexist language and gender-neutral language.

> It is important, then, to distinguish between the terms *gender-neutral* and *nonsexist*. *Gender-neutral* is a linguistic description: a gender-neutral term is formally, linguistically unmarked for gender: *police officer, domestic violence, flight attendant* in place of gender-marked *policeman, wife battering, stewardess*. *Nonsexist* is a social, functional description; a nonsexist term works against sexism in society. (Frank & Treichler, 1989, pp. 17-18)

A term may be both gender-neutral and nonsexist. However, nonsexist terms are not always gender-neutral nor are gender-neutral terms always nonsexist terms.

Gender-neutral terms are not always the most appropriate terms for identifying what has occurred or what is occurring. The term domestic violence presents an example of a gender-neutral term that is not non-sexist. "[Domestic violence] hides the male agency and focuses our attention on the places where men beat their wives and children, dwellings, disguising violent acts as well as erasing the male agents" (Penelope, 1990, p. 209). Accuracy in language is important; when gender-marking is relevant, it should be done. Domestic violence may be technically accurate but the vast majority of domestic violence remains wife battering and child beating.

Inclusive language resembles both gender-neutral language and nonsexist language but is not identical with either gender-neutral or nonsexist language.

> Inclusive language—the term preferred rather than nonsexist—is a way of expressing the concern for using words that do not exclude, or express bias against individuals or groups regardless of gender or attributes such as race or color. Inclusive language recognizes the value of all human beings and does not limit our understanding of God. (Withers, 1984, p. 7)

Like both gender-neutral and nonsexist language, inclusive language is a response to the domination of the language and experience of certain people, in this case women, by the language and experience of other people, in this case men (Withers, 1985b, p. 652). Like nonsexist language, inclusive language in-volves issues of oppression, at the very least the oppression of women. Like gender-neutral language, inclusive language involves linguistic usage and struc-ture that, at the very least, is not sexist. Encompassing both gender-neutral lan-guage and nonsexist language, inclusive language can be described as truly ap-propriate language usage: if women are intended, say so; if men are intended, say so; if human beings are intended, say so.

Accordingly, inclusive language involves more than pronoun adjustment (such as changing from the so-called generic "he" to any other options, such as he/she, she/he, she or he, he or she, or s/he) or finding appropriate alternatives for the so-called generic "man" (such as firefighter in lieu of fireman). Although both pronoun adjustment and the finding of other appropriate alternatives are important, still more subtle changes also are needed. Inclusive language is one way by which that which has been linguistically hidden can be brought into the open. "Inclusive language is born in the struggle of those who are linguistically invisible as they come to the recognition that their linguistic invisibility reflects and perpetuates the exclusivist bias of the institutions of society" (This-tlethwaite, 1985, p. 558).

Developing one's use of inclusive language involves learning new linguis-tic habits. These new habits need to include ways of speaking, writing, and lis-tening that include and encourage. New linguistic usage also would include ex-amining current linguistic usage for discrimination that occurs in various of ways, both conscious and unconscious, and taking appropriate action, that is, regular self-critique. With these new linguistic habits also comes a realization of the power that language possesses. Learning to use inclusive language takes continuing effort in order for such usage to become a thoughtful habit. "Inclu-sive language is not a place to be reached, but a reaching toward language that respects and includes as many dialects as possible" (Moore, 1985, p. 611).

However, any use of the English language that contributes to sexism needs to be made more inclusive if the goal is a more equitable world. Any local dia-lect that excludes in harmful ways needs to be changed, to become more inclu-sive. Such changing does not necessarily mean that the entire dialect would be eliminated. Also, since languages change over time, what is being suggested is that change needs to be a little more controlled, consciously moved in directions that promote a more inclusive culture. "The desire of those working for inclu-sive language is not for domination, but for true diversity in which no one image or model decides the nature of God or of the human person" (Russell, 1985, pp. 592-593).

Education and Religious Education

In this study, the view of education adopted involves helping students to learn, encouraging students to want to learn, to explore new areas, and to make connections between ideas as well as between learning and life. "The students are alive, and the purpose of education is to stimulate and guide their self-development" (Whitehead, 1967a, p. v). Education also involves the entire per-son—the physical, the mental, the emotional, even the spiritual. Far too often, traditional education has focused on some particular area, such as the cognitive, and neglected the other aspects of students. "I lay it down as an educational axiom that in teaching you will come to grief as soon as you forget that your pupils have bodies" (Whitehead, 1967a, p. 50).

Education is not necessarily the same as either indoctrination or instruction. Indoctrination, as in the production of useful citizens who without much thought follow the leaders, is not education. In indoctrination, truth is hidden; accuracy and honesty are sacrificed for "the good of society," "national security," or some other "higher purpose." The students are given only one side, the side of those in control, in a positive manner; other positions are either ignored or presented in a negative manner. Instruction has more to do with information from a "big bucket" (belonging to the instructor or leader) being poured into a "little bucket" (belonging to the student or follower). Instructors impart their knowledge to the students; the students absorb as much as they can, perhaps ask some questions of clarification, and then repeat the information back to the instructors at the appropriate times.

While some indoctrination or instruction may be appropriate in some circumstances, when either instruction or indoctrination or some combination of the two become the controlling aspect(s) in an educational system, then true education has been lost. For example, in learning about the ideals of the United States of America, indoctrination may have a limited role; in learning the technical details in a subject, e.g. anatomy, instruction is appropriate. In any case, the ideas memorized or taught by means of instruction or indoctrination are not to be left to themselves; they need to be incorporated into the rest of the student's life, or at least the attempt should be made to do so. "The whole book [*The Aims of Education*] is a protest against dead knowledge, that is to say, against inert ideas" (Whitehead, 1967a, p. v).

Religious education can be described in a number of ways, some of which are educational in the manner set forth above, some of which fit better with instruction or indoctrination, and some of which are better described in other ways.[1] One approach to describing religious education is organizational. From such a perspective, religious education is viewed as any program contained in the education budget of a religious organization and designated as having an educational function in that organization. Religious education also can be viewed as training or instruction of the young in the ways of the community of faith and reaffirming and exploring the tradition by the adult membership, whether or not such training occurs as part of an organized, budgeted program or not. Or, religious education can be viewed as inclusive of all education, a view stated here by Alfred North Whitehead:

---

1. Seymour & Miller (1982) present descriptions of five modern approaches to Christian education: religious instruction, faith community, spiritual development, liberation, and interpretation. These approaches exemplify a variety of teaching and learning styles, including different combinations of the styles mentioned in this chapter, and can be found in non-Christian religious education.

> The essence of education is that it be religious. Pray, what is religious educa-tion? A religious education is an education which inculcates duty and rever-ence. Duty arises from our potential control over the course of events. Where attainable knowledge could have changed the issue, ignorance has the guilt of vice. And the foundation of reverence is this perception, that the present holds within itself the complete sum of existence, backwards and forwards, that whole amplitude of time, which is eternity. (Whitehead, 1967a, p. 14)

To say that all education is religious is not to say that any institution claim-ing to be an educational institution really is one. Much of what claims to be edu-cation turns out to be, upon closer examination, heavily dependent upon instruc-tion or indoctrination, neither of which are, by description, proper forms of education when allowed to dominate the learning process. A properly accredited high school may be educational, for example, in a legal sense, but if the school relies primarily on some combination of indoctrination and instruction, then the school would not be educational in the sense described above. However, any situation or system promoting education in the way described can be described also as religious education.

This inclusive approach to religious education, as suggested by Whitehead, involves helping people find ways of living that promote integrity, ways of liv-ing that encourage healthy lives and relationships, and ways of living that help persons to overcome the isolation and selfishness that are moving the human species towards extinction. "Duty" and "reverence," as suggested by Whitehead, involve concern for our obligation to learn, to exercise our knowledge to the best of our abilities throughout our daily lives, and to realize that every moment is sacred and in some way connected with every other moment—past, present, and future.

> You can interpret the past in terms of the present. The present is all that you have; and unless in this present you can find general principles which interpret the present as including a representation of the whole community of existents, you cannot make a step beyond your little patch of understanding. (Whitehead, 1974, p. 82)

> The only use of knowledge of the past is to equip us for the present. No more deadly harm can be done to young minds then by depreciation of the present. The present contains all that there is. It is holy ground; for it is the past, and it is the future. (Whitehead, 1967a, p. 3)

An inclusive approach to religious education is an appropriate description of the type of religious education adopted for this investigation.[2]

---

2. Inclusive approaches to religious education have been presented previously. For example, Durka and Smith (1976a &1976b) used process theology as a basis for their work with models of God, including how those models develop, how such models influ-ence other aspects of life, and how the models can be altered. Giltner (1985) presents a range of issues in which religious education has a role to play, including language, peace,

[A] genuinely religious education will be one that rages against all separation, division and injustice. It will also be one that includes the voices of persons everywhere in attempting the educational work of interpreting the totality of human reality and experience. (Withers, 1985b, p. 652)

Transformation, Theoretical Constructs, and Perception

There are people for whom "inclusive language," "transformation," and other such words are triggers for a fear response. Yet transformation can be a neutral concept. The hoped-for transformation could be one in which the person changes from an atheist to a theist. Transformation would seem to involve radical change, whether that change be rapid or slow, from one way of being in this life to a significantly different way of being in this life. If one of the goals of religious education is to help persons grow in their faith, altering their way of living this life in some fashion, and if language is one of the means by which change is encouraged, then the language used in the religious education process should be supportive of the goal. Those who claim to be inclusive, and yet continue with primarily masculine references to Divinity, may well be deceiving themselves and inhibiting their own project, belying their own claims. On the other hand, inclusive language aids in the pursuit of wholeness, in the transformation from a divided person to an integrated one.

In this study, theoretical constructs that can aid in fostering inclusive language usage are offered. Theoretical constructs may sound too abstract, too divorced from the real world. However, the hope is that the theoretical constructs proposed and used in the following chapters will prove to be useful tools for the analysis of how and why the resistance to change occurs and for the presentation of grounds for possible transformation. The hope also is that these theoretical constructs will prove to be appropriate labels for recurring life patterns and will help in understanding more of the language-thought-perception-behavior complex in which each of us is involved.

Perception in this study is used in a comprehensive way. Events that occur outside of human bodies are received by human beings. Some of these events will be consciously known; many will register with the senses. However most of

---

and domestic violence. Giltner says that "religious education has a great future as an advocate for inclusivity and mutuality in God's great world" as women reconceptualize both religious education and their role in it (Giltner, 1985, p. 2). Harris (1988) suggests an inclusive approach to religious education based upon, though not limited to, women's experience and involving spirituality.

The role of inclusive language in religious education has been of some concern over the years. Russell (1976) is an early example of this concern, focusing on nonsexist interpretation of the Bible. In the 1980's, Withers (1980 &1984) and Westerhoff (1985) are examples of the concern for inclusive language in religious education. More recently, Groome (1991) has provided a brief and very good summary of the reasons for inclusive language as well as some suggestions for implementing inclusive language.

The main differences between these previous approaches to inclusivity and this study are the kinds of explanatory theory being used, the amount of emphasis placed on that theory, and the attempt to link the theory with practice.

the events will be felt unconsciously. The received information is interpreted, and information "goes out" from the perceivers. The relationship of this output to language usage and the relationship of the language usage to behavior are especially relevant in this study. Perception involves a complex set of relationships that includes language, thought, and behavior.

Whitehead, Whorf, and Piaget

Ideas from the works of Alfred North Whitehead, Benjamin Lee Whorf, and Jean Piaget are helpful in illuminating some of the issues involving sexist language and inclusive language. The views of these three thinkers appear to be generally compatible and to be capable of reinforcing each other. No defense of the views proposed by Whitehead, Whorf, and Piaget is given in this study. Although legitimate questions about various features of their positions, or indeed about their positions as a whole, can be raised, this is not the place to discuss such questions. Being convinced that their respective views are generally accurate descriptions of reality, their basic insights are helpful in dealing with patterns which recur in real life, in leading to more accurate worldviews, and in exploring the relationships among language, thought, perception, and behavior.[3]

Certain labels have come to be associated with the work of each of the three thinkers used in this study, some self-affixed, some given from without. In *Process and Reality* (1978, passim) Whitehead called his approach "philosophy of organism" and the "organic philosophy," but "process philosophy," "process theology," "process-relational philosophy," and "process thought" are other terms that have been used for this approach. *Philosophy of organism* and *White-headian thought* are the two most frequently occurring labels in this text. Whorf (1956) described his view as "the principle of linguistic relativity." The "Sapir-Whorf hypothesis," "the Weltanschauung hypothesis," and "linguistic determinism" are other terms that have been applied. *Linguistic relativity* and *Whorfian thought* are the two most frequently used terms in this text. Piaget claimed he was studying "genetic epistemology," that is, the biological origins and biological development of human thought, especially scientific-mathematical thought; Piaget's work also has been described as "developmental psychology," "child development," "early childhood education," "cognitive psychology," and "cognitive development." *Genetic epistemology* and *Piagetian thought* are the two most frequently used labels in this study.

Assumptions and Concluding Remarks

The following assumptions contribute to the foundation of this study:

---

3. An element of irony occurs in using the thought of three male thinkers to discuss and explore the case for inclusive language. Nonetheless, the use of Whitehead, Whorf, and Piaget can help illuminate the development of sexist language, the resistance to inclusive language, and the possibilities for language's becoming more inclusive.

(a) Society in the United States is usually sexist.

(b) The English language as usually practiced is sexist.

(c) The sexist usage of the English language contributes to, promotes, reinforces, and helps to cause the sexist thinking, perception, and behavior that occurs in individuals and is prevalent in society.

(d) The views of Whitehead, Whorf, and Piaget are mostly accurate descriptions of reality.

(e) Religion and religious education in their various forms are intertwined with society and, therefore, tend to be sexist in their language, belief, and practice.

If all five assumptions are accurate, then the theories of Whitehead, Whorf, and Piaget can help lay the bases for a coherent and consistent account of how sexist language interacts with sexist thought, sexist perception, and sexist behavior. Further, the theories of Whitehead, Whorf, and Piaget can also provide a basis for transforming religious education through the use of inclusive linguistic habits.[4]

In this study insights from the perspectives of Whitehead, Whorf, and Piaget are applied to the issues of sexist language and inclusive language. The perspective of each thinker is used to discuss the stubbornness of sexist language, to set out the possibilities for implementing inclusive language, and to analyze the

---

4. The assumptions and the interplay among them raise many interesting topics, many of which are beyond the scope of this study. However, following are some comments upon the first three assumptions.

The complex relationship between the English language, sexism, and English-speaking culture has been discussed in many places. Julia Penelope in *Speaking Freely* (1990) has presented an especially thorough discussion of this complex relationship. Penelope shows a variety of ways in which the English language is sexist and supports sexism. Two of these are the passive voice in sentence construction and the use of euphemistic or ambiguous terms.

According to Penelope (1990, pp. 149-166), the passive voice is frequently used to hide the agent, the oppressor. For example, the sentence "wars are waged" does not say by whom—*men* wage the wars. "Wars are waged" suggests that wars are inevitable or merely the result of circumstances and that *men* merely respond as best they can. Or, compare the following sentences: (a) "A woman was raped by five men." (b) "Five men raped a woman." The first sentence subtly suggests that the woman was somehow involved in being an active agent in the rape, whereas the second sentence is much clearer about who did what to whom. The passive voice very often is a subtle way in which the grammar of the English language supports sexist thought, perception, and behavior.

Penelope (1990, pp. 250-252) also suggests that "incest" is a euphemism and does not convey the true horror of the situation—the betrayal of trust, the abuse of power, and the emotional and physical harm done to the child(ren) involved. "Incest" suggests that the sex was mutual and voluntary. Neither of the other possible alternatives, "father rape" and "daughter rape," are any better since both terms are ambiguous. The former suggests that the male parent was the victim; the latter suggests the rapist was someone other than a male relative. Penelope states that this inability in English to "create a word or a phrase that expresses accurately, fully, and explicitly the horror of the violence men do to children" indicates an important characteristic of English: "the English language is fully exposed as collaborating in the protection of men" (Penelope, 1990, p. 251).

paradigmatic story presented at the opening of Chapter 1. The three perspectives used in this study demonstrate the importance of language in the thought, behavior, and perceptions of humans.

Chapter 3
Whitehead's Philosophy
of Organism and Language

In this chapter Whitehead's philosophy of language is presented, with an application of those views to sexist language and inclusive language and to the situation of children growing up in a patriarchal society. This chapter is organized as follows: (a) a presentation of five notions from Whitehead's philosophy of organism; (b) a presentation regarding Whitehead's theory of expression; (c) a presentation of Whitehead's more general views on language; (d) a description of language in the philosophy of organism; and (e) an application of a Whiteheadian philosophy of language to the issue of sexist language in general and to that issue in relation to young children in particular.

Five Whiteheadian Notions

Following are presentations regarding five concepts important in Whitehead's philosophy of organism: actual entities, the ontological principle, the principle of relativity, the power of the past, and novelty. These notions are especially relevant to the later discussions about language.

Actual Entities
The philosophy of organism is based upon an event-metaphysics, and these basic events are called "actual entities" or "actual occasions."

> 'Actual entities'—also termed 'actual occasions'—are the final real things of which the world is made up. There is no going behind actual entities to find anything more real. They differ among themselves: God is an actual entity, and so is the most trivial puff of existence in far-off empty space. But, though there are gradations of importance, and diversity of function, yet in the principles which actuality exemplifies all are on the same level. The final facts are, all alike, actual entities; and these actual entities are drops of experience, complex and interdependent. (Whitehead, 1978, p. 18)

Actual entities combine in various ways, from quarks to whales, from protozoans to redwoods, from electrons to humans, from dirt to chairs.

Actual entities are "occasions of experience" containing both mental and physical feelings. "Every occasion of experience is dipolar. It is mental experience integrated with physical experience" (Whitehead, 1958, p. 32). Furthermore, these experiences build upon each other. In the human being, these experiential integrations sometimes result in sense-perception and consciousness. Unconscious, nonsensuous perception forms the basis for sense-perception and consciousness (Whitehead, 1961b, pp. 228-229). Consciousness and sense-perception are derivations. Most experience is unconscious and primarily physical. "Consciousness is no necessary element in mental experience. The lowest form of mental experience is blind urge towards a form of experience, that is to say, an urge towards a form for realization" (Whitehead, 1958, p. 32).

The Ontological Principle

Ontology is the study of being, including such topics as the nature of being or reality as such, the kinds of beings that exist, the nature of actual being, and the nature of relations. From the perspective of the philosophy of organism, every reality refers to, and involves some configuration of, actual entities. Whitehead calls this view the ontological principle (Whitehead, 1978, passim).

> According to the ontological principle there is nothing which floats into the world from nowhere. Everything in the actual world is referable to some actual entity. It is either transmitted from an actual entity in the past, or belongs to the subjective aim of the actual entity to whose concrescence it belongs. (Whitehead, 1978, p. 244)

Whitehead is insistent. "Everything must be somewhere; and here 'somewhere' means 'some actual entity'" (Whitehead,1978, p. 46). Also, when looking for causes or explanations, one is looking for at least one actual entity and more likely some configuration or combination of actual entities; "actual entities are the only reasons" (Whitehead, 1978, pp. 19 & 24).

Further, all decision-making, at all levels, involves actual entities and "in separation from actual entities there is nothing, merely nonentity—'the rest is silence'" (Whitehead, 1978, p. 43). This decision-making involvement of actual entities also illustrates the interrelatedness of actual entities with each other. "An actual entity arises from decisions for it and its very existence provides decisions for other actual entities which supersede it" (Whitehead, 1978, p. 43).

According to the philosophy of organism, "everything is positively somewhere in actuality and in potency everywhere" (Whitehead, 1978 p. 40). In this quote, "everything is positively somewhere in actuality" refers to the ontological principle, that is, everything that *is* is either one or more actual entities or else is present in such; "in potency everywhere" refers to the principle of relativity.

The Principle of Relativity

In Whiteheadian thought, "relativity" refers to the potential of each entity to be involved in the development of each subsequent actual entity; that is, "every item of the universe, including all the other actual entities, is a constituent in the constitution of any one actual entity" (Whitehead, 1978, p. 148). This situation is not accidental but is inherent in the nature all actual entities.

Whitehead's principle of relativity gives rise to the importance of interrelatedness. In the philosophy of organism, every part of the universe is in some way, actually or potentially, related to every other part of the universe. "The philosophy of organism is mainly devoted to the task of making clear the notion of 'being present in another entity'" (Whitehead, 1978, p. 50). There are no completely isolated individuals, either actually or potentially.

> Connectedness is of the essence of all things of all types. . . . No fact is merely itself. The penetration of literature and art at their height arises from our dumb sense that we have passed beyond mythology; namely, beyond the myth of isolation. (Whitehead, 1966, p. 9)

Nor is there any mind-body dualism. "The universe, thus disclosed, is through and through interdependent. The body pollutes the mind, the mind pollutes the body. Physical energy sublimates itself into zeal; conversely, zeal stimulates the body" (Whitehead, 1974, p. 85). The physical, the mental, and the emotional are thoroughly interwoven. The physical is "the basis of our emotional and purposive experience" (Whitehead, 1966, pp. 114-115), yet some element of mental or emotional activity always is involved, however minimal such activity may be. "The philosophy of organism abolishes the detached mind. Mental activity is one of the modes of feeling belonging to all actual entities in some degree, but only amounting to conscious intellectuality in some actual entities" (Whitehead, 1978, p. 56).

Just as past experiences exercise various degrees of influence upon the development of human beings, likewise past actual entities do not contribute equal portions to each subsequent actual entity. In the process of integrating feelings, some feelings will be omitted. Whitehead acknowledges "degrees of relevance and negligible relevance" (Whitehead, 1978, p. 50); some feelings are more appropriate to a developing actual entity than are other feelings.

The Power of the Past

According to the philosophy of organism, the past exercises much influence on the present, especially through its role in the development of both simple and more complex individuals. One of the sources of this power of the past is in the sameness that occurs between previous events and subsequent events; sameness increases influence.

> [A]ny likeness between the successive occasions of a historic route procures a corresponding identity between their contributions to the datum of any subsequent actual entity; and it therefore secures a corresponding intensification in the imposition of conformity. (Whitehead, 1978, p. 56)

The power of the past is especially evident in the notion of repetition. "In the organic philosophy the notion of repetition is fundamental. The doctrine of objectification is an endeavor to express how what is settled in actuality is repeated under limitations, so as to be 'given' for immediacy" (Whitehead, 1978, p. 137). Repetition involves patterns of feelings being repeated. Repetition also involves actual entities ignoring novelty, or at least incorporating only minimal novelty into themselves. In some cases this means that actual entities do not exercise as much freedom as they could. With repetition, the power and influence of the pattern being repeated builds. With sufficient repetition, the pattern becomes a habit and correspondingly more difficult to alter; an intensity builds with repetition (Whitehead, 1978, p. 253). The more a habit is the result of intense repetition, the more difficult it becomes to alter that habit. Consistent patterns of repetition yield permanence; the appearance of changing events yield flux.

The power of the past is responsible for the stability of the present and can be quite controlling. Creatures with less freedom, less awareness of freedom, are more likely to repeat the patterns of the past. The ongoing repetition of previous patterns, can be and often is, such that changing those patterns in any significant way is very difficult.

Novelty

Amidst the interconnectedness and the power of the past mentioned in the preceding subsections, the philosophy affirms the possibility of novelty entering into the process. Two of the primary ways by which novelty occurs involve the role of freedom and the lure of the Divine. Both of these factors are discussed below.

While some philosophies suggest that interconnectedness automatically results in some form of determinism, Whiteheadian thought integrates the self-creative role of the individual within the network of connections that constitute reality. As part of the description of "freedom," Whitehead means the ability of an individual to contribute something, however minimal, to its own creation and to the future creation and self-creation of other individuals. This self-creative aspect is complicated; feelings and relationships are integrated in various ways with varying degrees of complexity. There is "a hierarchy of occasions of experience which are all of the same kind" differing only in the "degree of self-determination and hence also in their ability to make a novel synthesis of the relationships" (Griffin as cited in Regan, 1982, p. 17). Despite the power of the past, individuals have the ability to change.

> I used to play in the middle of the scrum. They used to hack at your shins to make you surrender the ball, a compulsory element—but the question was How you took it—your own self-creation. Freedom lies in summoning up a mentality which transforms the situation, as against letting organic reactions take their course. (Whitehead quoted in William Ernest Hocking "Whitehead as I Knew Him," *Journal of Philosophy*, 14 September 1961:512, cited in Hendley, 1986, p. 75)

"In the middle of the scrum," much occurs that is "compulsory." In the midst of reality much of what is done by individuals is forced or necessitated by events outside of the immediate control of the individual. The individual response, or the "how you took it," is an indication of the degree of freedom obtained by the individual involved. Each and every individual, from the simplest subatomic events to the most complex beings, has some degree of freedom.

As mentioned in the discussion on "actual entities," each entity is composed of mental and physical feelings or experiences. The combining of mental and physical feelings occurs throughout the various combinations of entities that occur, including human beings. Further, feelings and experiences are combined in ways that the individual is able to guide. Freedom involves the individual's being able to select from among the various experiences that are flowing into the developing individual. Freedom builds upon the mental feelings contained in each actual entity. The more complex the individual is, the more potential freedom to select from among the mental feelings is available and the more variable can be the response to physical experience.

Incorporating freedom into the system at the earliest stages, or in the logical foundations, of the philosophy of organism provides at least two positive conditions. The first condition is a more consistent philosophical system than those systems in which freedom, especially human freedom, is an "add-on" or afterthought of some sort, resulting in difficulties for those systems, for example assuming that nature strictly follows (Newtonian) laws and then trying to explain human freedom. Whitehead explains the dilemma of those taking that approach.

> Each molecule blindly runs. The human body is a collection of molecules. Therefore, the human body blindly runs, and therefore there can be no individual responsibility for the actions of the body. If you once accept that the molecule is definitely determined to be what it is, independently of any determination by reason of the total organism of the body, and if you further admit that the blind run is settled by the general mechanical laws, there can be no escape from this conclusion. (Whitehead, 1967b, p. 78)

The second positive condition provided by the incorporation of freedom into the foundations of the philosophy of organism is that it allows, without inconsistency, adequacy to the belief, which all humans presuppose in practice, that human beings are morally responsible beings.

> In defence of this notion of self-production arising out of some primary given phase, I would remind you that, apart from it, there can be no moral responsibility. The potter, and not the pot, is responsible for the shape of the pot. (Whitehead, 1959, pp. 8-9)

The Divine plays significant roles in Whitehead's philosophy of organism, and one of those roles is in presenting individuals with possibilities. In this role, the Divine "lures" the individual to choose an option deemed by the Divine to enhance the experience of the individual. In providing these possibilities, the Divine introduces novelty into both the life of the individual and the ongoing cosmological process. "Apart from God, there could be no relevant novelty" (Whitehead, 1978, p. 164). Further, the luring of creatures by the Divine goes on indefinitely, with adjustments made that take into account previous decisions. Individuals, perhaps especially human beings, are constantly being presented with new possibilities by the Divine.

> God's role . . . lies in the patient operation of the overpowering rationality of [God's] conceptual harmonization. [God] does not create the world, [God] saves it: or, more accurately, [God] is the poet of the world, with tender patience leading it by [the Divine] vision of truth, beauty, and goodness. (Whitehead, 1978, p. 346)[1]

---

1. In keeping with the theme of this study, within quotations the so-called generics will be replaced with appropriately inclusive language in brackets.

The philosophy of organism balances the power of the past, which is the basis of order and permanence, with novelty, as it occurs through individuals' choosing from among the possibilities presented in the feelings from the past and in the lure of the Divine.

> These various aspects can be summed up in the statement that *experience* involves a *becoming*, that *becoming* means that *something becomes* and that *what becomes* involves *repetition* transformed into *novel immediacy*. (Whitehead, 1978, pp. 136-137)

If there is too much novelty, chaos is close at hand; if there is too much order, progress is stifled, eventually unto the point of death. Sometimes the swing is towards conservation and "order," so that liberation is inhibited; sometimes the swing is towards liberation and novelty, so that tradition is minimized. "Thus understanding has two modes of advance, the gathering of detail within assigned pattern, and the discovery of novel pattern with its emphasis on novel detail" (Whitehead, 1966, pp. 57-58).

Expression and Language

In Chapter 2 of *Modes of Thought* (1966, pp. 20-41) Whitehead offers a 'theory of expression.' All forms of expression are part of the complex of events composing this cosmic epoch.

> Expression is the diffusion, in the environment, of something initially entertained in the experience of the expressor. No conscious determination is necessarily involved; only the impulse to diffuse. This urge is one of the simplest characteristics of animal nature. It is the most fundamental evidence of our presupposition of the world without. (Whitehead, 1966, p. 21)

The need for human beings to express themselves has resulted in various types of symbolism, the most apparent of which, from a human perspective, is language, spoken and written (Whitehead, 1959, p. 62).

Symbolism, to be sure, is widespread and not limited to language. Symbols come in many forms and tend to be aspects of experience that can be easily used to represent other aspects of experience. Symbols can be smells, images, written words, aesthetic experiences (Whitehead, 1978, p. 183). Sense-data is another form of symbolism (Whitehead, 1959, pp. 2-4).

While there are many types of symbolism, language is of central importance. "Language is the example of symbolism which most naturally presents itself for consideration of the uses of symbolism. Its somewhat artificial character makes the various constitutive elements in symbolism to be the more evident" (Whitehead, 1978, p. 182). A spoken word conveys not only cognitive content or thought. The sound of the word and the tone used in saying the word elicit feelings for consideration, and the feelings can easily vary from listener to listener. "The mere sound of a word, or its shape on paper, is indifferent. The word is a symbol, and its meaning is constituted by the ideas, images, and emotions, which it raises in the mind of the hearer" (Whitehead, 1959, p. 2). According to Whitehead, words serve as symbols for much more than thought. Triggering feelings for possible incorporation into experience is a more important function of words: "it is a mistake to think of words as primarily the vehicle of thoughts" (Whitehead, 1978, p. 182).

Language, as in words, strings of words, patterns of word usage, and the like, is thoroughly entwined in Whitehead's theory of expression and is, therefore, integrated in the combinations of events that make up the universe. Language is "the outstanding example of the way in which [humankind] has fabricated its manageable connections with the world into a means of expression" (Whitehead, 1966, p. 31).

General Theory of Language

Language is mentioned frequently in the writings of Whitehead. In this section, the following three topics involving language are discussed: (a) difficulties involved with language, (b) the subject-predicate form of expression, and (c) the value of language.

Difficulties Involved with Language

Three of the difficulties with language involve going beyond daily life, the illusion of precision promoted by science, and the fallacy of the perfect dictionary. Language has been, and continues to be, useful in dealing with daily human life. But when language has to deal with metaphysical principles, with novel thought, with issues like personal identity and other similar mysteries, problems arise (Whitehead, 1961a, pp. 163-164). In dealing with metaphysical issues, words have to be stretched beyond their ordinary usage (Whitehead, 1978, p. 4). Language focuses so much on the ordinary aspects of life that dealing with the extraordinary is not easily done. Whitehead suggests that the history of ideas is full of "the struggle of novel thought with obtuseness of language;" for example, even "[Plato] wrestles with the difficulty of making language express anything beyond the familiarities of daily life" (Whitehead, 1961a, p. 120).

The common expectation is that language expresses precisely what humans see, feel, think, and hear. One of the main contributors to this expectation is science. "[T]he radically untidy, ill-adjusted character of the fields of actual experience" are hidden by language "moulded by science, which foists upon us exact concepts as though they represented the immediate deliverances of experience" (Whitehead, 1967a, p. 106). The breadth, depth, and flow of experience tend to be hidden by "the neat, trim, tidy, exact world which is the goal of scientific thought" (Whitehead, 1961b, p. 22). However, language involves much more than the exactness suggested by science. Language involves meaning, both cognitive and emotional, of words, of grammatical forms, and of the meanings beyond the words and grammatical forms as occurs in great literature (Whitehead, 1961a, p. 226).

This ideal of exactness also has influenced philosophy. The most obvious example of this tendency has been the rise and the continuing power of analytic philosophy. Further, the view that human beings already have thought all the important thoughts and only that which has been thought is truly important.

> There is an insistent presupposition continually sterilizing philosophic thought. It is the belief, the very natural belief, that [humankind] has consciously entertained all the fundamental ideas which are applicable to its experience. (Whitehead, 1966, p. 173)

Another effect of the ideal of exactness has been the expectation that language serves as a perfect vehicle for delivering important thought.

> Further it is held that human language, in single words or phrases, explicitly expresses these [fundamental] ideas. I will term this presupposition, 'The Fallacy of the Perfect Dictionary'. (Whitehead, 1966, p. 173)

To the contrary, Whitehead suggests that "[l]anguage is thoroughly indeterminate, by reason of the fact that every occurrence presupposes some systematic type of environment" (Whitehead, 1978, p. 12). That is, each use of language is done within a context, and in order to understand completely what is said, one needs to be aware of more than merely the superficial aspects of that context. Being aware of the entire context turns out to be a very difficult task, especially when one realizes that the context is not stable. The precision of language is bound up in a knowledge of the various levels of changing contexts within which the language is used.

The Subject-Predicate Form of Expression

Whitehead points to subject-predicate language, a form of expression bequeathed to the Occident through the Greeks, as a form of expression that has had enormous influence on Western thought. Subject-predicate language has preserved and perpetuated the notion that there are isolated, individual bits of substance to which qualities adhere, and this notion has had effects on science and philosophy (Whitehead, 1978, pp. 77-79, 158-159, & 167). "All modern philosophy hinges round the difficulty of describing the world in terms of subject and predicate, substance and quality, particular and universal" (Whitehead, 1978, p. 49).

Whitehead clearly rejects the subject-predicate form of expression as a completely adequate description of reality (Whitehead, 1978, p. xiii). Although often pragmatically useful, the subject-predicate form of expression contains the assumption that enduring substances, with their essential qualities, are the final real things. This assumption conflicts with Whitehead's view of actual occasions as the final realities. Accordingly, the "subject-predicate mode of expression is wrong . . . when taken as a statement of fundamental fact instead of the abstraction that it is" (Olewiler, 1971, p. 95). When the abstract nature of the subject-predicate form of expression is forgotten, then the fallacy of misplaced concreteness occurs. Far too often philosophers have presupposed that language usage accurately reflects "the fundamental nature of things" (Olewiler, 1971, p. 27). The connections between language and reality need to be explored, not assumed.

Value of Language

While Whitehead does not hesitate to point out the negative aspects of a metaphysically misleading language, he also appreciates the contributions language has made to the development of humanity. These contributions are manifest in myriad ways. For example, language helps human beings to focus on certain patterns, aspects, or components in experience and to remember those patterns for future use; that is, language assists in the development of cognitive processes—"an articulated memory is the gift of language" (Whitehead, 1966, p. 33). Language is viewed as the clearest way by which human beings have come to express the relationships that they perceive in the world (Whitehead, 1966, p. 31). Language is crucial in remembering ideas, in developing abstract thinking, and in communication. The importance of language in human development is recognized by Whitehead.

> [T]he mentality of [humankind] and the language of [humankind] created each other. If we like to assume the rise of language as a given fact, then it is not going too far to say that the souls of [human beings] are the gift from language to [humankind]. The account of the sixth day should be written, [God] gave them speech, and they became souls. (Whitehead, 1966, pp. 40-41)

Whitehead recognizes a curious tension in language. Language enables progress because language can promote freedom of thought, abstracting to future possibilities, recalling the past, and imaginative leaps. Yet language also serves to hinder progress; language is basically a conserving process tending to preserve its tradition.

> The essence of language is that it utilizes those elements in experience most easily abstracted for conscious entertainment, and most easily reproduced in experience. By the long usage of humanity, these elements are associated with their meanings which embrace a large variety of human experience. Each language embalms an historic tradition. Each language is the civilization of expression in the social systems which use it. Language is the systematization of expression. (Whitehead, 1966, p. 34)

Language may "embalm" a tradition, but the embalming need not be permanent. Embalming of a tradition tends to inhibit the very freedom of thought that language sometimes encourages (Whitehead, 1966, pp. 34-35). However, preserving the past need not always be a hindrance to progress. Preserving the past may be necessary for some types of progress. Language can both aid the freedom of individuals and coordinate societal members: People who learn the same language tend to have similar values and worldviews; such commonalty tends to make cooperation easier (Franklin, 1990, p. 300). However, this preservation can become a block to creativity as well as an active force for returning to a past uncritically viewed. Language allows abstraction from the concrete, thereby providing potential escape from the embalming process, if that path is selected.

Language, thought, and civilization have grown together. The ability to abstract, to go beyond the present situation that language enhances, is an especially important factor in the development of both thought and civilization.

> Apart from language, the retention of thought, the easy recall of thought, the interweaving of thought into higher complexity, the communication of thought, are all gravely limited. Human civilization is an outgrowth of language, and language is the product of advancing civilization. Freedom of thought is made possible by language: we are thereby released from complete bondage to the immediacies of mood and circumstance. (Whitehead, 1966, p. 35)

In addition to contributing to the development of thought and civilization, language also reflects the various aspects of its culture of origin.

> Language is the incarnation of the mentality of the race which fashioned it. Every phrase and word embodies some habitual idea of men and women as they ploughed their fields, tended their homes, and built their cities. For this reason there are not true synonyms as between words and phrases in different languages. (Whitehead, 1967a, p. 66)

Language both provides a way by which a culture can be unified and presents possibilities for a culture to surpass itself. "But in an especial manner, language binds a nation together by the common emotions it elicits, and is yet the instrument whereby freedom of thought and of individual criticism finds its expression" (Whitehead, 1959, p. 68).

Language-using creatures have survived and, in the case of human beings, thrived. And this situation has developed despite the fact that language rarely if ever can be metaphysically exact. As Whitehead suggests, "no language can be anything but elliptical, requiring a leap of the imagination to understand its meaning in its relevance to immediate experience" (Whitehead, 1978, p. 13). Nevertheless, language is accurate enough to assist human beings in living everyday lives, in describing reality, in dealing with immediate experience; that is, language has helped human beings to survive. Language is used to highlight patterns of experience and to help language users deal with various patterns of experience that are encountered. "Yet the usages of language do prove that our habitual interpretations of these barren sensa are in the main satisfying to common sense, though in particular instances liable to error" (Whitehead, 1961b, p. 228).

Language, when involved in abstracting from reality, leads us away from concrete actuality and towards civilization, novel experiences, and organizing logical and aesthetic experiences (Whitehead, 1966, p. 39). Language contributes both to novelty and to survival: "the essence of language [is] that it must abstract from the particular situation—and its usefulness lies in ignoring the change of perspective as unimportant" (Olewiler, 1971, p. 84). Language tends to be so focused on abstracting and on survival that language has great difficulty in bringing "into consciousness the presuppositions of language and common-sense for which there is no language" (Olewiler, 1971, p. 3).

Language plays many roles in human life. Language enhances communication. Language can promote abstraction. Language has enabled the possibility of more freedom to develop. Also, language serves as a method of control, of organizing experience (a method that can be carried to extremes as in modern advertising). Still, as long as thought is more than language can exactly express and as long as there is a desire to express thought, then the potential is present for an individual or a society to go beyond the immediacy of ordinary life. When the multiple roles of language are forgotten, then problems in human life more easily can occur.

A Philosophy of Language

In this section the roles of language within a philosophy of organism are considered.[2] Within the philosophy of organism, language has a profound influence on thought and perception, and thereby on behavior. The remainder of this section discusses language in relation to the following notions: process and the ontological principle, the principle of relativity, propositions, perception, the interpretation of reality, and thought.

Language, Process, and the Ontological Principle

In the philosophy of organism there are two types of process: concrescence and transition (Whitehead, 1978, pp. 210-214). "Concrescence" refers to the internal process by which the various and sundry data are integrated by and within a developing individual; the many become one. "Transition" refers to the relationship between actual entities, the influence of one individual on subsequent individuals (Whitehead, 1978, pp. 210-214). In the process of concresence, language is part of the data that can be incorporated internally by actual entities.

The development of an individual is a complicated process. An individual receives data from a variety of sources—the immediate past, the distant past, and the Divine. An individual develops goals and purposes. These goals and purposes are partially received from God, partially from the past, and partially from its own self-creation; the proportions vary with the complexity of the individual involved. The more complex the actual entity is, the greater potential the entity has for making greater contributions to its self-creation. The past data and

---

2. In addition to Whitehead's own works, Stephen Franklin's book *Speaking from the Depths* (1990) and Betty Jane Olewiler's dissertation, *Whitehead's Philosophy of Language and the Whorfian Hypothesis* (1971), are used for the presentations in this section.

the criteria for incorporation are integrated into the next incarnation of that individual.

Language is one of the sources of data in this process. For language-using individuals, language influences the process of incorporation by virtue of being both part of the content and part of the criteria by which the data is evaluated; "both the pre-linguistic world and the world as shaped by language are present in the concrescing entity and lie open for inspection" (Franklin, 1990, p. 265).

Unchallenged, repetitious use of linguistic habits not only entrenches those habits more deeply but also limits the pool of alternatives available to individuals in their process of self-creation. However, linguistic habits can be challenged, and this challenging occurs in two general ways. Linguistic habits may be challenged directly, as when one person confronts another person regarding some usage of language. Linguistic habits may also be challenged indirectly, as when personal experience shows how it can feel to be a victim and to be treated as a non-person. Unfortunately, not every challenge will be overtly successful, but every challenge does contribute to possibilities for the development of subsequent individuals. Every challenge to linguistic habits contributes to the pool of alternatives available to individuals in their process of self-creation.

Language and the Principle of Relativity

> A precondition for experience is the involvement with the 'other', that is, with 'communication' in its broadest sense. In Whiteheadian terms, an actual entity begins its process of concrescence by incorporating other entities into itself as part of its very identity. . . . [T]he very possibility of language is built on the prior involvement with the other. (Franklin, 1990, p. 257)

According to this Whiteheadian principle of relativity, all events are related in some way to all other events, and there are wide varieties of ways by which this relatedness occurs. Past events contribute to present events, and present events form the basis for future events. Insofar as language, thought, perception, and behavior are complex sequences of events, these complex sequences of events are mutually influential. The more involved the relationships, the more mutual influence there will be; less intimacy tends to yield less influence.

Given the sort of interrelatedness mentioned previously, all past and current events, including language-events, are in some way and to some degree connected with and influencing every future event, whether these events are in the more distant future or the more immediate future. In Whiteheadian thought, both in the individual and in the species, once language emerges, it feeds back into thought. Perception and behavior both precede thought and language, chronologically and logically, and feed back into future thought and language, and so on.

Language, therefore, influences thought, perception, and behavior. If language that demeans, degrades, or excludes women is part of the initial data, and if sexist language has become part of the goals and criteria that help to sort the initial data, then the probability is high that sexist language will promote sexist thought, sexist perception, and sexist behavior. The connections are metaphysical and multicausal.

Language and Propositions

In classical Western thought, especially in the analytic tradition, a proposition is viewed as a purely verbal statement with a true/false value. Whitehead proposes a more expansive view of propositions, a view in which propositions are not limited to verbal statements. "A proposition . . . is a datum for feeling, awaiting a subject feeling it" (Whitehead, 1978, p. 259). Whitehead suggests that propositions are lures for feeling; that is, propositions are potentials that serve as one possible way of going beyond the given past and of creating novelty (Olewiler, 1971, p. 72). "The proposition is the possibility of that predicate applying in that assigned way to those logical subjects" (Whitehead, 1978, p. 258). A proposition is a meaning, although it also is true that a statement can express or evoke an indefinite number of meanings or propositions (Griffin as cited in Regan, 1982, p. 18). A verbal statement is one expression, but not the only possible expression, of a proposition.

Whitehead rejects the classical view that language can adequately express propositions (Whitehead, 1978, p. xiii). From a practical perspective, linguistic expression cannot adequately deal with the constantly changing circumstances which affect the proposition being considered. A perfect correspondence between a verbal expression and its referent is highly unlikely. From a metaphysical perspective, adequate expression of a proposition requires complete cosmological knowledge; because such knowledge is most unlikely, perfect understanding of any particular expression of a proposition remains impossible. "Apart from a complete metaphysical understanding of the universe, it is very difficult to understand any proposition clearly and distinctly" (Whitehead, 1958, p. 68).

Propositions do not appear ex nihilo; "according to the ontological principle, every proposition must be somewhere" (Whitehead, 1978, p. 147). That somewhere, according to the ontological principle, is some actual entity or entities. "Every proposition is entertained in the constitution of some one actual entity, or severally in the constitution of many actual entities" (Whitehead, 1978, p. 147). Propositions are to be found in the internal processes of individuals. Possibilities that are not found in earthly individuals are to be found in the Divine.

The primary function of propositions is to provide options during the self-development of the actual entity, "for feeling at the physical level of unconsciousness" (Whitehead, 1966, p. 186). In other words, in the process of internal integration by the actual entity there are many possibilities from which to choose. Propositions are an important source of possibilities for the individual. Further, propositions are of two types, conformal or non-conformal. Conformal propositions result in repetition and fact, while non-conformal propositions result in novelty, including error (Whitehead, 1978, p. 187). In addition, propositions work in all levels of complexity throughout this cosmic epoch; they are not limited to human beings. ""Not just human psyches or animal psyches, but also actualities at every level, incorporate propositions" (Griffin as cited in Regan, 1982, p. 18).

Propositions are necessary though not sufficient for language. For Franklin (1990), "any linguistic act has two sides: (A) the specified propositional prehension and (B) the language, that is, the sense perception of the squeaks or shapes" (Franklin, 1990, p. 258). Both (A) and (B) are within the self-development process of the individual. Linguistic statements cannot correspond to reality, yet such statements can still be "true insofar as they elicit into consciousness propositions that do" (Griffin, 1992, p. 124).

Language and Perception

According to the philosophy of organism, there is a stream of experience that is unconscious, very concrete, and pre-linguistic. This stream of experience is the vast majority of experience. The actualities involved in this stream are linked. New actualities develop out of past actualities, and time passes—concrescence and transition occur. This stream is reality and, based upon this reality, interpretations are made. Some data are incorporated into developing actualities, some data are not. The more accurate the interpretations, the better are the chances for surviving and thriving; the less accurate the interpretations, the less likely the chances for surviving and thriving.

There are two general types of perception according to the philosophy of organism: nonsensuous and sensuous. The former occurs constantly, necessarily, and usually unconsciously. The latter is commonly called sense-perception. The latter is based upon the former. Basic to Whitehead's philosophy of organism and his views on expression and language is the view that consciousness, thought, and language presuppose experience (Olewiler, 1971, p. 92). The type of experience presupposed is unconscious and nonsensuous. Human beings experience much more than they know; they know much more than they remember; and they consciously remember much more than they can say, as has been demonstrated in the relationship between hypnotism and memory.

Language serves as a way to highlight certain patterns that occur within the flow of experience. Permanent factors tend to be in the background of consciousness; variable factors are the attention getters. Over the centuries, the evolution of language has resulted in the focusing of language upon "the accidental aspect of accidental factors" (Whitehead, 1961b, p. 204). Language does not easily highlight background phenomena. "[T]hat which is metaphysically important remains in the background of thought and language, just because it is so important. What is important for conscious observation is the variable" (Olewiler, 1971, p. 22).

Language, once developed, feeds back into the experiential flow contributing to the emergence of actual entities, but language is one factor among many and is of variable importance depending upon the individual involved. Yet there remains some experience not very much influenced by language. For example, the odds are greatly against a naked mole rat, never having been directly involved with any language-using creature, to be very much affected by language. Nevertheless, language can, and often does strongly influence human perceptions. Franklin suggests that language possesses the ability to greatly influence human perception, sometimes to the point of controlling the makeup of the perceptions (Franklin, 1990, p. 295).

Language and the Interpretation of Reality

Interpretations of reality are based upon an abundant flow of data—entities, experiences, feelings—all of which is considered, consciously or unconsciously. Reality is far more than any finite individual can comprehend, and out of this welter of experience, an actual entity constructs a "work-a-day world," the world on which the entity focuses and in which the entity lives and experiences (Franklin, 1990, p. 297). Within the flow of reality, then, there are numerous possible work-a-day worlds or subrealities which can emerge (Franklin, 1990, p. 297).

Language influences the development of work-a-day worlds in human beings, yet the abundance of data comprising reality is not exhausted. "[While] language may shape and create the work-a-day world, it does not thereby eliminate Reality. Even though we are linguistic beings, we still have access to Reality in its pre-linguistic dimensions" (Franklin, 1990, p. 298). So, while human interpretations of reality are influenced by language, the abundance of data that comprises reality remains. "Whitehead's view [is] that experience is partially but not wholly structured by language because we have prelinguistic experience of reality that is not eliminated in the self-construction of a moment of experience" (Griffin, 1992, p. 124). Eventually language becomes part of the abundance of data from which work-a-day worlds are constructed.

For human beings, selecting a specific work-a-day world often is shaped by language since a work-a-day world arises out of prehensions involving propositions, and "the function of language is to elicit such propositional prehensions" (Franklin, 1990, p. 297). In the individual human being, a work-a-day world eventually reaches consciousness (Franklin, 1990, p. 297). Language serves as one guide in the construction of a language user's work-a-day world. According to Franklin (1990, p. 358), "there is an infinity of data at the first stage of each new entity which is simplified as the concrescence progresses, and . . . language is one of the factors guiding that entire development."

Language shapes and elicits propositional prehensions, of which sense perceptions are one type. Language shapes our sense perceptions in proportion as it shapes our propositional prehensions.

> [W]hen language guides the creation of a particular work-a-day world out of the Reality to be found at the first stage of concrescence, it is guiding the creation of *content* of that work-a-day world and is not merely providing a description of that work-a-day world. (Franklin, 1990, p. 297)

Language and Thought

While realizing the importance of language as a means of expressing thought and in the development of thought, Whitehead rejects the contention that language and thought are identical with each other (Whitehead, 1966, p.

34). He suggests two reasons for opposing the equivalence of thought with language. First, if the equivalence of thought and language were true, then translating from one language to another and providing alternative versions of sentences within the same language would be impossible. "[I]f the sentence is the thought, then another sentence is another thought. It is true that no translation is perfect. But how can the success of imperfection be achieved when not a word, or a syllable, or an order of succession is the same?" (Whitehead, 1966, pp. 34-35). Human experience in the United Nations indicates that some communication and understanding do occur. Accordingly, the equivalence of language with thought is not supported.

Second, Whitehead also points to the struggle of some human beings to express their ideas as evidence against the contention that "words and their order together constitute our ideas" (Whitehead, 1966, p. 35). If this contention were true, then there should not be any struggle involved in expressing our thoughts. Our human experience, perhaps most clearly seen in poets, indicates otherwise.

While language and thought are not equivalent, they do influence each other. For Whitehead, thought is possible without language, though not possible without some form of expression, in the form of some other type of symbolism or in behavior. "The notion of pure thought in abstraction from all expression is a figment of the learned world" (Whitehead, 1966, p. 36). Thought and language have shaped each other (Olewiler, 1971, p. 96). All of this is to suggest that while language is neither identical with thought nor completely adequate in representing thought, language and thought have influenced each other in important ways.

Concluding Remarks

Language shapes the way we perceive and interpret reality. Further, language also is a part of the content being perceived and interpreted. "Language is a part of the world. It is internal to the world. And it is one of the means whereby the world is presented to and introduced into the identity of the person using the language" (Franklin, 1990, p. 255). Language, in other words, contributes to the shaping as well as to the content of human thought, perception, and behavior.

Application to Sexist Language Issues

As indicated in the preceding discussion, language is thoroughly bound up with the metaphysical process. Also, language is both a product of and a contributor to the metaphysical process. In this section the results of the preceding section are applied both to the issue of sexism in language and to the situation of children growing up in a patriarchal society. In both applications the stubbornness of sexist language and the possibility of transformation to inclusive language are considered.

Language both contributes to and serves as an indicator of the world in which human beings live. Language conjures images, evokes emotions, integrates thoughts, expresses feelings, and more, though the influence and variety of functions differs from individual to individual. Language occurs within and contributes to a context. In a Whiteheadian metaphysics, the context is in flux. The flux is not always obvious, for example, when the same, or very similar, patterns of events are repeated. Additionally, the context can change in ways that may be viewed as progressive or reactionary, regressive or evolutionary. Some kinds of change are more complex than primarily physical change, or mere repetition.

Stubbornness

Language is one strand in the initial data that an individual considers; accordingly, sexist language usages would be part of the linguistic strand in the initial data. The more sexist language data, the more likely is the use of sexist language and other sexist actions. In the process of integrating data, selection occurs. Some data (feelings) are admitted; some data are omitted. The selection process is in part guided by language. If deeply rooted linguistic habits are sexist and these habits are fed by varieties of sexist data from the past (both the distant past and the near past), then the odds of continuing sexist language interpretation and usage increase. Sexist perceptions at all levels will contribute to sexist language.

By force of repetition, sexist language promotes sexist thought, perception, and behavior. Repetition involves habits; the more repetition that occurs, the more ingrained the habit becomes; hence, the more sexist language is used, the more difficult will it be to alter the habit of using sexist language. Propositions, that is, possibilities, are expressed through language; also, propositions are presented at an unconscious level. If most propositions, conscious or unconscious, are sexist, the likelihood is increased that the language, thought, perception, and behavior related to these propositional feelings will be sexist.

Language contributes to both the standards of evaluation and the content being evaluated by those standards. Therefore, sexist language contributes in two general ways to sexist perception, thought, and behavior: (a) by being part of the initial data and (b) by being part of the guiding criteria by which data are selected for incorporation by the self-creating entity. The more sexist language is included in the various aspects of the process, the more difficult the sexist language will be to remove. Sexist language from daily conversation, advertising, television, and other sources are part of the initial data, as are nonsexist, inclusive language, images, and other events. In Anglo-American culture the quantity of sexist events, past and present, still far outweighs the quantity of nonsexist events. The power of the past is strong, and sexist language is still very much part of the repeating past.

As long as the proportion of sexism, including sexist language, to nonsexism in the data remains lopsided in favor of sexism, then the likelihood is strong that sexism will remain entrenched. Repetition enhances the power of the past. For example, in contemporary United States, television remains overwhelmingly sexist and the amount of time spent watching television by children exceeds all other sources (perhaps more time watching television than school, homework, and church time combined). Accordingly, the odds will favor the continued use of sexist language. If television were to become more inclusive, then the probability of inclusive language gaining acceptance would increase. Sexist language is stubborn and very much a matter of deep-seated individual habits, reinforced by the dominance of sexist language in the initial data from the past.

Transformation

A basis for transformation from sexist language to inclusive language can be found within a philosophy of organism. Due to the realities of freedom, creativity, and self-determination, language is flexible. Language-using creatures can alter their linguistic usage; inclusive propositions can be selected, new patterns of repetition can be developed resulting in inclusive linguistic habits beginning to take root. Inclusive propositions can be presented and selected at an unconscious level.

Inclusive elements, including inclusive language, are present in the initial data, even if the quantity of these elements pales in comparison with the sexist elements. Still, those traces of inclusivity remain available for selection by the individual. Since human beings are capable of making choices that contribute to their own self-creation, it is possible for a person to choose to use inclusive language and to begin developing inclusive linguistic habits. But such a choice, conscious or unconscious, is not easily made; the past weighs heavily on the present. The development of a "critical consciousness" can begin by means of continuing attempts, which can become more successful over time, to select inclusive language. Self determination presents an ongoing opportunity for reducing sexist language and increasing inclusive language usage.

Whitehead's theory of expression and philosophy of language are part and parcel of Whitehead's metaphysics. Given the connectedness of each sequence of events with each other sequence of events, then what occurs in language influences thought, perception, and behavior in some way. The reverses are all equally true as well. For example, behavior affects thought, language, and perception. The military focuses on changing behavior, thereby affecting the thought, language, and perception of its personnel. Sexist language helps produce and reinforce sexist perceptions, sexist thought, and sexist behavior. If inclusive language were used in homes, schools, and churches, then the process would include much more inclusive language data. Such an increase of inclusive language in the initial data would then influence the selection process itself. Even a little inclusive language helps some—as a proposition, a lure for feeling, a potential. Any instances of inclusive language in the process provide possibilities for the use of inclusive language in an individual's daily life. The more inclusive linguistic events that occur, the greater the likelihood of actualizing inclusive language by the individual in an environment, or at least the greater the likelihood of attempting inclusive language in one instance, and maybe in a second.

Reducing sexist data and changing sexist language habits will require a focus of attention, of consciousness aimed at changing the initial data and the environment, and by encouraging, luring, persuading the young child to use inclusive language by means of role-modeling, conversation, and other techniques not themselves sexist in nature.

The Story

Habits begin to develop early. Unconsciously the girls and boys to whom Joanmarie Smith refers in the narrative example used at the beginning of this study have developed patterns of linguistic usage and interpretations of reality that are sexist. The girls, when imagining themselves to be boys, chose careers that males tend to have—careers that are stereotypically considered to be "high prestige" careers, such as the law or medicine. Most of the boys either could not imagine being a girl or would rather be "nothing" or "dead" than be a girl. The power of the past—parents, schools, churches, and more—has provided sexist data through which reality is viewed.

Children can be influenced in more inclusive directions. In order to influence children in a more inclusive manner, or at least to have a chance at such altering, the initial data and the criteria need to be changed. Altering initial data and criteria can be done consciously as well as unconsciously. Attention needs to be directed towards decreasing the quantity of sexist data and increasing the quantity of inclusive data. Further, the sexist data of the past—data that continues to be available to self-creating individuals—need to be brought to consciousness in order to be critiqued and dealt with properly.

The past, with all of its sexist data, is part of each integration of feelings by human beings; so also are instances of inclusive events. The degree of relevance of the data depends upon many factors, but the power of the past, of repetition, is difficult to alter. Given that all events are part of the system and influence the process, the higher the frequency of sexist events (including sexist language events), the higher the probability that a child will develop sexist language, attitudes, and behavior. However, positive experiences are never completely obliterated, though they can be deeply buried or swamped by negative experiences. Inclusive language experiences may be a small stream in the flux of language experiences, but inclusive language experiences can be utilized at any point in this process. Propositions, whether sexist or inclusive or neutral, are metaphysically available at all times, though some are more easily attainable at certain times than at others.

Repetition—that is, the power of the past—promotes sexist language and is one of the supports of patriarchy. Flowing alongside the sexist data from the past is a stream, perhaps only a trickle, of nonsexist or inclusive data that is more or less accessible. Those who are able to take from this stream are able to begin building new patterns of repetition, new linguistic habits. The children in the paradigmatic story have been raised in the milieu of the sexist past; their future access to inclusive language is unknown, but their access can be improved. Further, children in the present and the future can be presented with more inclusive language, thought, perception, and behavior.

Chapter 4
Whorf's Principle of Linguistic Relativity

Benjamin Lee Whorf was born, raised, educated, and worked in the capitalist, comfortable milieu of Boston and Cambridge (Massachusetts) in the early 20th century. Whorf graduated from the Massachusetts Institute of Technology and then had a very successful career as a fire safety inspector for the Hartford Insurance Company. His inquiring mind did not let him rest and led Whorf to the study of Amerindian languages, especially Hopi. In the early 20th century, Whorf, who had become a noted amateur linguist, proposed what he called a "new principle of (linguistic) relativity."

> We are thus introduced to a new principle of relativity, which holds that all observors are not led by the same physical evidence to the same picture of the universe, unless their linguistic backgrounds are similar, or can in some way be calibrated. (Whorf, 1956, p. 214)

Between then and now, Whorf's proposal has generated much heat, if not much light. On the one hand, Whorf's critics call Whorf's defenders "mystics, romantics, anecdotalists" (Fishman, 1982, p. 3). On the other hand, defenders of Whorf tend to accuse Whorf's critics of vulgarization, oversimplification, reductionism, and distortion, and of not having really read Whorf (Fishman, 1982, p. 3).

The purposes of this chapter are two: (a) to discuss and clarify Whorf's principle of linguistic relativity and (b) to apply this interpretation of the principle of linguistic relativity to the issue of sexist language and to the situation of children growing up with gender biases. Towards fulfilling these twin purposes this chapter is organized as follows: (a) a presentation of Whorf's principle of linguistic relativity, (b) a brief discussion of the main difficulties involved in dealing with Whorf, and (c) applications of Whorfian thought to sexist language issues.

Linguistic Relativity

Whorf believes that language has a profound effect upon thought, perception, and behavior. The influence of language is inversely proportional to a person's or group's awareness of the power of language. The following discussion of linguistic relativity relates Whorf's views on language to the following topics: (a) background phenomena, (b) meaning, (c) thought, (d) perception and worldview, (e) behavior, (f) freedom and control, and (g) critical consciousness.

Language and Background Phenomena

> The fact that we talk almost effortlessly, unaware of the exceedingly complex mechanism we are using, creates an illusion. We think we know how it is done, that there is no mystery; we know all the answers. (Whorf, 1956, pp. 250-251)

Whorf suggests that language is an example of background phenomena. Background phenomena are those aspects of life that are taken for granted and usually unconscious, at least until they are explicitly called into the foreground in some manner. Background phenomena are so common that they apparently are irrelevant to daily life, until some disruption occurs that focuses attention on their importance (Whorf, 1956, pp. 209-210). Background phenomena, sometimes referred to as common sense, are multifaceted and include cultural, scientific, and personal factors; further, common sense tends to be unaware that the use of language involves a system of cultural factors (Whorf, 1956, p. 67). Specifically, with respect to language, each language seems simple enough to its native speakers because the native speakers are unaware of the organization of their language (Whorf, 1956, p. 82). However, as learning another language proves, the simplicity assumed by a native speaker often is not the case for a nonnative speaker learning that language.

As part of his presentation about language as background phenomenon, Whorf discusses natural logic (Whorf, 1956, pp. 207-211). Natural logic makes two assumptions that Whorf believes need to be questioned. The first assumption is that persons who have been fluent in their native language since infancy are to be considered experts on that language, its grammar, and other relevant matters (Whorf, 1956, p. 207-208). The other assumption is that different languages are parallel methods for expressing the same thought, that languages involve superficial differences covering the same or very similar thought processes (Whorf, 1956, p. 207-208). According to Whorf, neither assumption is supported by the evidence.

Whorf points out that the background nature of language tends to place language beyond the conscious awareness and power of speakers and that speakers tend to assume the universality of their own language traits, imposing such traits on other languages instead of understanding the other languages in their own environments (Whorf, 1956, p. 211). Whorf also suggests that agreement on some subject matter, as in the negotiation of a trade treaty between nations, is not the equivalent of knowledge of the various linguistic processes involved in reaching that agreement (Whorf, 1956, p. 211). The background nature of language tends to mask these assumptions and problems; focusing on language allows these assumptions and problems to be noticed.

Language and Meaning

For Whorf, language and meaning are closely related. "Meaning will be found intimately connected with the linguistic: its principle is symbolism, but language is the great symbolism from which other symbolisms take their cue" (Whorf, 1956, p. 42). And within the realm of the linguistic, meaning (or sense) results much more from the patterns of relations between words and morphemes than from the words and morphemes themselves (Whorf, 1956, p. 67). Whorf points to music and children's use of language as examples of the importance of patterns in the development of meaning (Whorf, 1956, p. 261). He also makes it clear that words in and by themselves are not speech, that speech involves patterns of words and rhythms, and that patterns are more important than individual words (Whorf, 1956, p. 253). According to Whorf, only a few individuals (primarily mathematicians and scientific linguists) have experienced "in one fugitive flash, a whole system of relationships never before suspected of forming a unity" and the resulting "flood of aesthetic delight" (Whorf, 1956, p. 254).

The patterns of meaning need not be consistent across languages. In English, for example, the patterns focus on subjects and predicates, substance and attributes. Other patterns are possible and do occur. For example, Whorf notes that Amerindian languages demonstrate coherent language structures in which subjects and predicates are not to be found (Whorf, 1956, p. 242).

Language and Thought

While Whorf believes that language has great influence on thought, he does not believe either that language is equivalent to thought or that thought is possible without language. Whorf's principle of linguistic relativity suggests that each language analyzes reality in its own way. Two viewers of the same events may give interpretations of those events. If those viewers are speakers of the same language, they can compare notes and probably understand most of what the other says. However, if the viewers are speakers of different languages, then there is some possibility of communication if their different languages are able to be correlated in some fashion (Whorf, 1956, 212-215 & 250-253). Now, if thought and language were strictly identical; that is, if each thought were perfectly represented by one and only one piece of language and could only be so represented by that one piece of language, then the possibility of any calibration would be nil. Since Whorf indicates that some calibration is possible, as his own experiences with Amerindian languages demonstrates, language and thought, in his view, are not equivalent to each other.

Whorf also suggests, after all of his studies in linguistics, that language is not the only way the individual has of expressing thought.

> My own studies suggest to me, that language, for all its kingly role, is in some sense a superficial embroidery upon deeper processes of consciousness, which are necessary before any communication . . . and which also can, at a pitch, effect communication without language's and without symbolism's aid. (Whorf, 1956, p. 239)

However, Whorf is fully aware of the importance of language in the development and expression of thought. Whorf believes, for example, that the progress of science, especially since 1890, involves more than different modes of thought. The progress of science, perhaps more importantly, involves fresh ways of talking about the data (Whorf, 1956, p. 220). Whorf says, "the study of language . . . shows that the forms of a person's thoughts are controlled by the inexorable laws of pattern of which [that person] is unconscious" (Whorf, 1956, p. 252). And perhaps the most important influence of language on thought is demonstrated in the effects that language has upon human perception.

Language, Perception, and Worldview

According to Whorf, one's language is an essential component not only in the expression of one's worldview but also in the very fabric of that worldview. "We dissect nature along the lines laid down by our native languages" (Whorf, 1956, p. 213). Language provides the primary way of organizing experience; on this point Whorf is most emphatic.

> [L]anguage first of all is a classification and arrangement of the stream of sensory experience which results in a certain world-order, a certain segment of the world that is easily expressible by the type of symbolic means that language employs. (Whorf, 1956, p. 55)

> We cut nature up, organize it into concepts, and ascribe significances as we do, largely because we are parties to an agreement to organize it in this way— an agreement that holds throughout our speech community and is codified in the patterns of our language. The agreement is, of course, an implicit and unstated one, BUT ITS TERMS ARE ABSOLUTELY OBLIGATORY. (Whorf, 1956, pp. 213-214)

This perception and worldview development occurs at both individual and collective levels. For example, on the individual level, there is the episode of the "Coon cats" (Whorf, 1956, pp. 261-262). Apparently Persian cats of a certain type were, in parts of New England, known as "Coon cats." One of the results of the application of the label "Coon cats" was the emergence of the opinion that these cats were the result of interbreeding between raccoons and cats. People who believed this theory pointed out how much their "Coon cats" resembled raccoons. Biologists were consulted, gave their views on the impossibility of interbreeding, and were not believed. And while those who believe in "coon cats" may be more naive than those who accept the authority of the biologists, nevertheless both groups of individuals have something in common. As Whorf says:

> In more subtle matters we all, unknowingly, project the linguistic relationships of a particular language upon the universe, and SEE them there, as the good lady SAW a linguistic relation (coon = raccoon) made visible in her cat. . . . But without the projection of language no one ever saw a single wave. We see a surface in ever changing undulating motions. (Whorf, 1956, p. 262)

Not only are ordinary people affected in this way by language, but also are professionals: "[S]cientists as well as ladies with cats all unknowingly project the linguistic patterns of a particular type of language upon the universe" (Whorf, 1956, p. 263). For example, Whorf points to the influence of language on the development of Western physics, especially in the notions of substance and attributes, of subjects and predicates, and of absolute space and absolute time. The Newtonian worldview has yielded vast amounts of useful data and has been a key factor in the development of human society, especially Occidental culture. However, as Whorf notes: "Newtonian space, time and matter are no intuitions. They are recepts from culture and language. That is where Newton got them" (Whorf, 1956, p. 153).

Whorf was aware of the developments in physics that the subject-predicate form of language does not accurately describe. Such descriptions apparently can be done more appropriately in the symbols of mathematics. Whorf, a linguist, suggested another way of expressing the new discoveries in physics—in the language of the Hopi. This language emphasizes subjectivity, vibration, relationships, and motion as opposed to objective atoms moving in absolute space and time (Whorf, 1956, pp. 55 & 78-85). "For, as goes our segmentation of the face of nature, so goes our physics of the Cosmos" (Whorf, 1956, p. 241). Habitual thought involves patterns of words as well as the give and take between the language and the culture involved. According to Whorf, Standard Average European languages (including English), things, bodies, substance and matter have priority; in Hopi, events have priority (Whorf, 1956, p. 147).

Language and Behavior

Whorf provides illustrations of the connection between language and behavior from his fire-safety experience (Whorf, 1956, pp. 135-137). For example, individuals smoked cigarettes around "empty" gasoline drums—the word "empty" having more power than the fact that the fumes remain in empty gasoline drums, even though gasoline fumes are more flammable than gasoline itself (Whorf, 1956, p. 135). In another situation, "spun limestone" was used as an insulation in a wood distillation process. This insulation was not protected from either excessive heat or from contact with the flame. However, the fumes from the distillation process chemically interacted with the limestone resulting in acetone, a flammable substance. When a fire did occur, the limestone burned. Whorf suggests that *limestone*, ending as it does with the word *stone*, encouraged actions on the part of the workers that allowed unsafe conditions to develop. After all, since stones are not flammable, limestone should not be flammable (Whorf, 1956, pp. 135-136).

Whorf also discusses the connection between the behavior of the Hopi and their language. The Hopi language is oriented towards events that are to come. Much of the daily life of the Hopi people is spent preparing for these future events (Whorf, 1956, pp. 148-152). In a manner quite similar to the fire-safety examples mentioned above, Whorf believes Hopi behavior is strongly influenced by their language (Whorf, 1956, p. 148). This attention to the effect of language on behavior is one of Whorf's most important contributions. "Whorf was primarily responsible for bringing this issue to our attention. He argued strongly that radical differences in linguistic structure led to radical differences in thinking, and hence to corresponding differences in behavior" (Lakoff, 1987, p. 329).

Language, Freedom, and Control

Whorf suggests that language, being a complex and massive system, can adapt to that which is new only at a slow pace (Whorf, 1956, p. 156). Language can be affected by innovations, but the effects tend to be small and take a long time to become widespread and effective. Being slow to change, language "limits free plasticity and rigidifies channels of development" (Whorf, 1956, p. 156).

Indications of the more creative side of language also can be found in Whorfian writings. For example, children are constantly repatterning their "language," though adults do not allow this behavior to continue unchecked and force the children back into the dominant language of the household, and the society if the two languages are different (Whorf, 1956, p. 261). Even scientific progress, Whorf suggests, has been partially the result of the use of language upon experience and evidence, thus indicating that language is not totally inhibiting (Whorf, 1956, pp. 220-221). Similarly, the development of poetry and of "teen music" can be cited as use of language which regularly pushes on the linguistic system.

Language can be used in novel and helpful ways as well as in controlling and stifling ways. On the one hand, teachers need to be aware of these ways in which language can be used in order to be able to model the type of language they wish students to learn. On the other hand, students, especially young children, could be encouraged in their creative uses of language, perhaps to write poetry or to develop secret codes and then to compare these uses with the more traditional uses. Teachers can help students to pay close attention to their developing linguistic usage in order to strive for a balance between order and novelty.

Language need not be limited by the patterns of words involved; for Whorf, meaning exceeds any particular expression of language due to the "connection of ideas" among words (Whorf, 1956, pp. 35-36). Likewise, Whorf's model of the Scientific Linguist (Whorf himself) provides an example of a person being able to get out of the worldview promoted by that person's native tongue; in the study of a truly foreign language, "we are at long last pushed willy-nilly out of our ruts" (Whorf, 1956, p. 244). Whorf's fire-safety inspection experience also provides a model of paying close attention to one's native language and overcoming the strong suggestions made by that language. While language provides limitations, these limitations can be overcome.

Language and Critical Consciousness

> Whorf is trying to persuade his readers to allow themselves to develop a hybrid consciousness, a multilingual consciousness, in order that they may learn, that they may see more than they have been able to see until now. And he is not asking them to renounce everything they have known up until now, except in parody. He respects science and religion and does not want to destroy either. (Schultz, 1990, p. 147)

Developing a critical consciousness involves a number of interacting factors. A critical consciousness involves becoming aware of the power of language, especially the power that one's native language asserts over both the individual, as in the fire-casebook examples, and the society (Whorf, 1956, pp. 135-137 & 244). Developing a critical consciousness involves becoming aware of one's linguistic habits and subjecting those habits to ongoing scrutiny. Developing critical consciousness promotes humility towards languages other than one's own and encourages cross-cultural and cross-linguistic studies, both of which in turn contribute to one's own intellectual and spiritual growth (Whorf, 1956, pp. 216-219; Rollins, 1980, pp. 70-76).

Humpty Dumpty, in talking with Alice, says that either you "master" words or they will "master" you (Carroll, 1992, pp. 295-299). Humpty chose to be in control of the language he used and thereby to use words as he wanted rather than being controlled by the language. Humpty Dumpty's arbitrary use of words would not be endorsed by Whorf, but Humpty Dumpty's other point would be supported by Whorf: Those who are unaware of the power of words are more easily controlled by words. That is, the more unconscious a person's linguistic habits are, the more control those habits are likely to assert over the person—to strongly influence how that person perceives the world, thinks about the world, and behaves in the world. A person who accepts a language in an uncritical manner and develops linguistic habits unthinkingly is much more likely to be at the mercy of that language. Conversely, an intentional, aware critical user of the same language will have more freedom with respect to thought, perception, and behavior.

Whorf's principle of linguistic relativity involves two notions. One notion is that a person's native language will exercise a controlling influence over that person's thought, perception, and behavior in proportion to the unconscious acceptance of, the habitual use of, and the lack of critical consciousness towards that language. The other notion is that no one language or culture has the complete objective Truth. Both persons and societies need to be aware of the different ways in which language controls and influences, as well as the ways in which language provides opportunities for liberation. Both persons and societies need to be aware of the ways in which diverse languages and cultures view reality. The development of a critical consciousness is necessary if linguistic control is to be challenged.

Difficulties in Dealing with Whorf

Whorf's principle of linguistic relativity has been subject to many critiques since its advent. In this section some of the main problems that occur in dealing with Whorf's principle of linguistic relativity are discussed under the following topics: (a) interpretations of Whorfian thought, (b) linguistic relativity as linguistic determinism, (c) challenging dogmatism, and (d) Whorf's own dilemma.[1]

---

1. One difficulty in dealing with "linguistic relativity" is deciding who is to receive the credit or the blame for developing the concept. One view is that Whorf alone is responsible for the principle of linguistic relativity (Rollins, 1980, p. 65). More frequently, the influence of Edward Sapir, a teacher and a colleague of Whorf, is acknowledged in the common label for linguistic relativity, the Sapir-Whorf Hypothesis.

Some scholars have suggested that the views that Whorf promoted can be found in the work of a variety of sources. Miller (1968) and Penn (1972) provide sketches of the history of linguistic relativity, suggesting that this tradition of thought is complex and traces back at least to John Locke: "Thus Locke can be considered as the earliest proponent of the Whorf (Alfred) Korzybski hypothesis which holds that the way people name

Interpretations of Whorfian Thought

Whorf's "new principle of [linguistic] relativity" has been interpreted in a surprising number of ways since its introduction. One interpretation says that linguistic relativity is 'linguistic determinism', "an extreme [version] asserting the dependence of thought on language" (Penn, 1972, p. 10); that is, the view that language completely dominates a person's, or a society's, thought, perception, and behavior (Feuer, 1953). Another interpretation is the view that language has minimal influence upon a person's thought, perception, and behavior (Kay and Kempton, 1984), "a mild [version] suggesting some influence of linguistic categories on cognition" (Penn, 1972, p. 10). Yet a third interpretation of Whorfian thought suggests that Whorf's primary goal is to promote awareness and appreciation of cultures other than the English-speaking, Occidental one in which Whorf lived (Fishman, 1982). Other interpretations of Whorfian thought can be found in Black (1959), Fishman (1960 & 1980), Penn (1972), Bloom (1981), Lakoff (1987), Butt (1989), Muhlhauser & Harre (1990), and Schultz (1990).

There appear to be two primary reasons for this wide variety of interpretations given to Whorf's principle of linguistic relativity. One reason involves Whorf's own style of writing and the complex way in which he views the role of language. The other reason involves Whorf's notion that no one culture or language has a monopoly on the Truth and that any culture can learn from any other culture. In the next section the first reason is considered in a discussion of linguistic determinism. The second reason is considered in the section entitled "Challenging Dogmatism."

Linguistic Relativity as Linguistic Determinism

Whorf's principle of linguistic relativity is very frequently interpreted as being the same as linguistic determinism. Linguistic determinism is the view that language completely controls the way a person, or a society, thinks, perceives, and interprets the world. If linguistic determinism were true, then a number of negative consequences follow. If these consequences are shown to be

---

situations influences their behavior relative to the situations" (Penn, 1972, p. 43). Sometimes Whorf is considered as being in the tradition of Johann Georg Hamann, who proposed a form of linguistic relativity that closely resembled linguistic determinism (Penn, 1972, pp. 53-56). Sometimes Whorf is viewed as in a direct line of descent from Johann Gottfried Herder; in this tradition, a multi-lingual, multi-cultural world is favored, "little peoples" and "little languages" are to be respected and valued; "the universal is a fraud, a mask for the self-interest of the dominating over the dominated" (Fishman, 1982, p. 8). Sometimes Whorf is considered to be most directly in the tradition of Wilhelm von Humboldt whose hypothesis suggests that "the worldview of one people differs from that of another people to a hitherto unheard-of degree" (Penn, 1972, pp. 19), reflecting the internal structure(s) of the language(s) involved, and sometimes language determines or is equivalent to thought (Penn, 1972, pp. 19-22). The problem in sorting out the tradition of linguistic relativity and Whorf's place in that tradition indicates the difficulty in interpreting Whorf and linguistic relativity.

inaccurate, then linguistic determinism is not true. And if linguistic relativity is the same as linguistic determinism, then linguistic relativity would also be shown to be untrue.

The two consequences most often mentioned can be found in the translation argument and the worldview argument. In the translation argument, if linguistic determinism is true, then there are completely separate linguistic universes and between such universes translation, including cross-cultural knowledge, is not possible. However there are instances of cross-cultural knowledge and of translation, of which Whorf's own work among Native American languages and cultures is an example. Therefore, linguistic determinism is not true (Feuer, 1953, pp. 94-96).

The worldview argument says that linguistic determinism is directly connected with the metaphysical view that different languages yield different worldviews. If linguistic determinism were true, then each language could express one and only one worldview. However, different worldviews can be expressed in the same linguistic family; for example, in the European languages the very different worldviews of Newton, Descartes, Hume, and Hegel have been expressed (Black, 1959, pp. 235-236). Further, different languages can express the same worldview. Therefore, linguistic determinism must not be true (Feuer, 1953, pp. 89-90).

Some interpreters of Whorf do not agree with the claim that Whorf's principle of linguistic relativity is the same as linguistic determinism. Fishman says: "Whorf never proposed that all aspects of grammar must inevitably have direct cognitive impact" (Fishman, 1960, p. 336). According to Muhlhauser & Harre, neither Whorf nor Sapir "espoused a thesis of strong determination from an independent language to a dependent human form of experience" (Muhlhauser & Harre, 1990, p. 2). Furthermore, "Whorf claimed only that language influenced the classification of what is perceived" (Muhlhauser & Harre, 1990, p. 2). If one does not accept the equivalence of linguistic determinism with linguistic relativity, then the translation and worldview arguments are not successful when used against linguistic relativity.

Critics and defenders agree that Whorf himself contributed to the confusion surrounding the interpretation of his principle of linguistic relativity (Olewiler, 1971, p. 137; Schultz, 1990, pp. 5-6); "no statement can be found in Whorf's writing which clears up the ambiguity as to which assertion (extreme or weak) he intended to be making" (Penn 1972, p. 13). Also, Kay and Kempton note that Whorf made sweeping claims, which would then be qualified (Kay & Kempton, 1984, pp. 75-77). While Whorf never explicitly affirmed linguistic determinism, he did make suggestions in that direction (Schultz, 1990, pp. 14-18). The following quotations indicate how linguistic relativity interpreted as linguistic determinism can be can be taken from the writings of Whorf.

[a] Thus our linguistically determined thought world not only collaborates with our cultural idols and ideals, but engages even our unconscious personal reactions in its patterns and gives them certain typical characters. (Whorf, 1956, p. 154)

[b] We cut up and organize the spread and flow of events as we do, largely because, through our mother tongue, we are parties to an agreement to do so, not because nature itself is segmented in exactly that way for all to see. (Whorf, 1956, p. 240)

[c] [T]he study of language . . . shows that the forms of a person's thoughts are controlled by the inexorable laws of pattern of which [she or he] is unconscious. (Whorf, 1956, p. 252)

By focusing upon these and similar quotations, a linguistic determinism interpretation of Whorfian thought is possible. However, a more careful reading of such quotations reveals qualifiers. In quotation [a], the words "collaborates," "engages," and "typical" serve as qualifiers. In quotation [b], "largely" serves as the qualifier. In quotation [c], an ambiguity occurs in the phrase "inexorable laws of pattern;" patterns can vary from situation to situation. If Whorf had used qualifiers more obviously, then the deterministic version of linguistic relativity would not be easily supported.[2]

A strong view of linguistic relativity may be accepted, without accepting linguistic determinism. This strong view suggests that the influence of language varies with a person's unawareness of the potential influence of language. Further, a variation on the translation argument can be used as support for a strong version of linguistic relativity. Many translations are easy, but many are not. Difficulties in translation serve to support Whorfian thought because such difficulties indicate that thought is not identical from one language to another. The actual problems that do occur in translation support a strong yet nondeterministic version of linguistic relativity (Whorf, 1956, pp. vii-viii). The translation argument works against linguistic determinism but does not work on all interpretations of linguistic relativity.[3]

---

2. I suspect one reason that many thinkers focus on linguistic determinism is that it is an easy target. Deductive claims are much easier to deal with, usually to disprove, than are inductive claims. Whorf, I suggest, was making inductive claims which analytics and positivists, then and now, have trouble accepting since such claims tend to be more complicated.

3. Bloom (1981) provides additional support for a strong, yet nondeterministic, view of linguistic relativity. Bloom compares counterfactual thinking in Chinese with counterfactual thinking in English. Considering "a state of affairs known to be false . . . for the purpose of drawing implications as to what might have been the case if that state of affairs were in fact true" is much easier to do in English than in Chinese (p. 14). Chinese lacks structures that enable handling of counterfactual situations. Bloom concludes that the results of his study support the Whorfian thesis that linguistic structures do strongly influence thought (pp. 29-60).

Challenging Dogmatism

Whorf's assertion of the powerful influence language tends to have on thought, perception, and behavior elicits reactions as much emotional as rational. Whorf has been called a practical joker, a sleight-of--hand artist, and a reveler in terror and glee (Schultz, 1990, p. 18). Whorf has also been accused of being overly religious and too mystically oriented (Schultz, 1990, pp. 10-12). One of the primary sources for this name-calling, as well as for the very diverse interpretations and evaluations given to Whorfian thought, can be found in Whorf's challenging dogmatism.

Whorfian thought challenges attitudes of superiority, whether the attitudes are racial or cultural or intellectual. Whorf challenged, in his own time, some of the reigning paradigms. In psychology, Whorfian thought challenged behaviorism; in philosophy, especially philosophy of language, the views of Frege, Russell, and the logical positivists were challenged (Bloom, 1981, p. 4). Whorf also opposed the "Nazi theories of Aryan superiority" (Lakoff, 1987, p. 330). Whorf further believed that Occidental civilization could learn from the so-called "less advanced" cultures, and such an attitude was very rare during the era in which Whorf lived (Lakoff, 1987, p. 330). In insisting on real dialogue between cultures, Whorf challenges the West's search for a single, univocal Truth (Schultz, 1990,p. 143). If Whorf is accurate, then there is no guarantee that humans will ever discover the absolute truth.

> And this is the essence of linguistic relativity: when meanings can vary to the degree we have discussed, and when there is no 'privileged form of representation'—no repository of universally relevant meanings—then there is no *one* world and no *one* reality. (Butt, 1989, p. 72)

Whorf even challenges the notion that perfect translations between languages, cultures, and thought systems are always possible (Lakoff, 1987, pp. 322-328). In forcefully raising the possibility that some differences between language may be incommensurable, Whorf challenges the belief that all languages and cultures are equivalent or can be assimilated into one primary language or culture; that is, all languages do not necessarily lead to American English. In the tradition of Copernicus, Marx, Darwin, and Freud, Whorf is pointing out blinders humans have put on themselves and encouraging both awareness and appreciation of other perspectives (Fishman, 1980, pp. 25-27). The Whorfian claim that human knowledge is dependent upon unknown linguistic factors also challenges the scientific basis of Western society. "In short Whorf (like Freud) impugns our objectivity and rationality" (Fishman, 1960, p. 326).

Whorf involves his audience in a process apparently designed to undermine the dogmatism of positivistic science (Schultz, 1990, pp. 28-43). The integration of loopholes, more or less obvious, throughout his writings is part of Whorf's method (Schultz, 1990, pp. 27-28 & 59-79). In dealing with the Boston and Cambridge audience of the '20s and '30s, Whorf indulges in some skillful rhetoric to promote his views. In supporting linguistic diversity, Whorf begins by presenting attitude his audience would not like. This attitude involves showing the audience how controlling and dominating language can be. Then Whorf would, tactfully yet forcefully, suggest that speakers of SAE (Standard Average European) languages have such an attitude toward so-called primitive languages. So, the audience is caught either disliking itself or needing to change its attitude (Schultz, 1990, pp. 22-24).

Whorf wants his English-speaking audience to begin to understand alien grammars and cultures without co-opting or assimilating those grammars (Schultz, 1990, p. 142). Whorf even uses crude drawings to assist in this task, to help to show "that understanding cannot be reduced to verbal translation alone" (Schultz, 1990, p. 99). Whorf also opposes false dilemmas. One is not limited to either universal impersonal truth or individual error, science or religion. There is a unified, multidimensional truth to be discovered (Schultz, 1990, pp. 43-47). Whorf's methods are intended to lead "his readers to draw the conclusions for themselves, to admit in spite of everything that there are more things in heaven and in earth than are dreamt of in their positivistic science" (Schultz, 1990, pp. 47-48).

Whorf's attempt to present noncanonical notions in a materialist-reductionist context contributes to the problems in interpreting the principle of linguistic relativity; "to argue holistically within the discourse of positivist science can *only* be interpreted as inconsistency" (Schultz, 1990, p. 18). So, Whorf tries to convince his audience, by means of various devices, that the so-called nonliterate, or illiterate, cultures have intrinsic and extrinsic value. Whorf lures his audiences into a trap in which they then become the "primitives" while the Native American speakers become the "heroes," and only by becoming a "scientific linguist," that is by developing a deep appreciation of and for other languages and cultures, can a "primitive" become a "hero." "Whorf moves back and forth between Native American languages and English in an effort to demonstrate experientially, without defining verbally, what a multilingual consciousness is like" (Schultz, 1990, p. 88).

In citing examples from both his fire safety experience and his study of Hopi in support of the effect of language on behavior, Whorf suggests that language can strongly influence behavior. To make such a suggestion is to challenge the superiority exerted by human beings over one another and the control we claim to have over ourselves. Whorf challenges humans, individually and collectively to deal with the fact that we are neither as in control nor as powerful as we think we are. No matter how smart we think we are, individually and collectively, we can learn from others, even those stereotyped as inferior. Linguistic relativity was, and is, an attempt to counteract negative attitudes and establish fair attitudes towards nonliterate cultures (Kay & Kempton, 1984, pp. 65-66).

Whorf's Own Dilemma

For Whorf a conflict was created as his upbringing, education, and success with the Hartford Insurance Company interacted with his linguistic studies. Whorf was caught "in a comfortable, complacent world of capitalist success," "cursed with a surplus of vision" that resulted in his questioning his own comfortable existence, and yet just could not leave Hartford (Schultz, 1990, p. 151).

Being trapped between Hartford and the Hopi contributes to the inconsistencies, both real and imagined, in Whorfian thought.

Whorf develops a "Galilean Language Consciousness"—involving fundamental awareness of change, diversity, dialogue, mutual illumination and enrichment, and opposition to repression (Schultz, 1990, pp. 49-97). Further, Whorf encourages the development of a "hybrid consciousness, a multilingual consciousness," which in turn will yield greater depth and richness of vision (Schultz, 1990, p. 147). He wants others to grasp this vision, to work towards a merging of science and religion, and to develop a critical consciousness that applies everywhere; the critics miss the vision (Schultz, 1990, p. 152). Whorf encourages his audiences to appreciate, without assimilating or co-opting, very different languages and cultures. "But it is exactly this point that Whorf's critics cannot accept" (Schultz, 1990, p. 142). A dialogical relativism of the sort proposed and practiced by Whorf "eludes the grasp of 'normal' philosophy, which is no doubt why 'normal' philosophers so fear it" (Schultz, 1990, p. 153). Those critics who interpret Whorf as proposing either linguistic determinism or some trivial influence of language on thought are caricaturing Whorf as well as missing the point. Perhaps they cannot deal with being a "primitive," being caught by their own so-called objectivity. Whorf appears to be caught between his traditional upbringing and his vision, but he begins working towards making his vision more real. Whorf's critics do not share Whorf's vision of developing a critical consciousness.

Trying to discover a consistent, univocal statement of deductive certainty in Whorfian thought will not be successful nor would such an effort be faithful to Whorf's own intention. Perhaps, instead of applying an emotionally pejorative label like "inconsistency," linguistic relativity should be considered multivalent, and if Whorfian material is taken out of context, then distorted interpretations can be expected. Whorf contributes to the confusion surrounding his writings; yet, "the whole of Whorf's writings testify to the hope, indeed, the insistence, that through studying different languages, we may gain better insight into the deeper processes of consciousness" (Olewiler, 1971, p. 137).

Applications of Linguistic Relativity

In this section the preceding discussions of Whorfian thought are applied to the stubbornness of sexist language, the possibility of transformation, and the narrative example presented at the beginning of this study.

Stubbornness

According to linguistic relativity, the interrelationships among language, perception, and behavior are complex and pervasive. Whorf focuses on the influential role that language plays in perception and behavior, a role that often goes unnoticed because language is a background phenomenon. Whorfian thought supports the notion that the language used, whether by an individual or by a society, can, and usually does, exert a significant influence on the worldviews that develop as well as on the behavior of the individual or society using that language. Accordingly, a person or a society that uses sexist language will be more likely to think, perceive, and behave in sexist ways than one who does not. Sexist language contributes to all forms of sexist behavior, some visibly violent behavior (rape, wife-beating) and other more subtle damaging behavior (unequal pay; glass-ceilings).

Further, the power of language runs deep. Linguistic habits begin to develop early and to be embedded in the life of the individual. The language a child hears is plentiful (estimated at 1/2 million clauses by age 4), fluent, and well-formed (Halliday as cited in Regan, 1988b, pp. 19-23). The more the language is used and reinforced, the more established the language becomes (Lamb cited in Regan, 1988b, p. 8). The more established the linguistic habits become, the more difficult they are to alter, even when the linguistic habits conflict with some views of the speaker.

Surprising stubbornness

Perhaps some of the best examples of the stubbornness of sexist language come from modern admirers of Whorfian thought. There are individuals who accept much of what Whorf said, especially regarding the power of language, but who apparently continue to use sexist language. For example, both Halliday and Lamb acknowledge the strong connections among language, meaning, thought, culture, and perception (Regan, 1988b, passim). According to Halliday (as cited in Regan, 1988b, pp. 14-15), language is a representation of reality, linguistic structures connecting the world outside with what goes on inside. Yet Halliday and Lamb's language usage is full of the so-called generic "he," and this usage illustrates the stubbornness of sexist language even in persons who acknowledge the influence of language (Halliday and Lamb as cited in Regan, 1998b, pp. 9, 26, 38, 40, 45, 47, 69, & 78).

An even more pronounced example of the power of sexist language occurs in Muhlhauser and Harre (1990). These authors support a type of linguistic relativity. They spend some pages discussing "what Sapir and Whorf really said" (Muhlhauser & Harre, 1990, pp. 2-8), and most of their book is devoted to supporting linguistic relativity. Muhlhauser and Harre even have included a chapter entitled "He, She, or It: The Enigma of Grammar and Gender" (Muhlhauser & Harre, 1990, pp. 228-247). In this chapter the authors defend the use of the so-called generic "he" and "man" as grammatically correct in certain circumstances. Further, the authors contend that language is merely a junior partner in the quest for sexual equality.

The authors also state that many of the feminist concerns are confusions that can be straightened out with proper understanding, and this point is made in a patronizing style. "We are strongly inclined to the view that the muddles that have excited the ire of certain feminists are almost wholly confined to academic writing, particularly in the human sciences and philosophy" (Muhlhauser & Harre, 1990, p. 231). The irony is that their own theory should tell them that since language influences thought, sexist language promotes sexist thought. Unfortunately, patriarchy is embedded so deeply that sexist language, unless blatantly insulting or disgusting, is not considered "bad." The tone of their chapter is condescending and suggests that, according to Muhlhauser and Harre, the problems of sexist language are mostly "muddles" that can be cleared up; to put the matter crudely, if you girls will just calm down and let experts explain the situation to you properly.

Transformation

"Unfortunately, or luckily, no language is tyrannically consistent. All grammars leak" (Sapir, 1949, p. 38). If the interpretation of linguistic relativity presented in this study is more accurate than not, then there is hope in overcoming the stubbornness of one's native language. A Whorfian basis for transformation is developing critical consciousness. This development can occur by means of learning other languages or by paying close attention to one's own language or doing both. The Whorfian emphasis on learning other languages and cultures supports the move towards diversity now occurring in educational systems throughout the United States. Learning new languages, especially non-SAE languages, enhances the possibility of developing a critical consciousness. Likewise paying close attention to one's own language, both in one's personal linguistic usage and in the linguistic usage of others, can enhance the development of a critical consciousness. In some situations a shock to one's linguistic system can trigger the start of such a consciousness. In other situations one can escape the influence by linguistic habits, as Schultz (1990) noted and Whorf practiced, by means of being lured into an appreciation of diverse cultures and languages.

Transformation from sexist language to inclusive language would involve processes similar to the processes used in developing a critical consciousness. More specifically, the introduction of inclusive language into early linguistic development would assist in altering thought, perception, and behavior at both individual and societal levels. Bringing language into critical consciousness and developing inclusive linguistic habits would result in more comprehensive thought, perception, and behavior.

The Story

From the perspective of linguistic relativity, the children in the paradigmatic story have been raised in a society in which the linguistic filters have promoted perception and behavior that encourages males while neglecting and discouraging females. As long as the background phenomenon, in this case the pervasiveness of sexist language, is accepted uncritically, then sexist language will continue to dominate, contributing to sexism in society, while inclusive language will remain underdeveloped and little used.

Given that linguistic habits develop early, using inclusive language from the beginning of a child's life would help to instill in the child the beginnings of more appropriate perception and behavior. Using inclusive language in early childhood also would help prepare the child for expanding inclusiveness in thought, perception, and behavior as the child grows. Further, socializing the child in an inclusive manner would enhance the process of developing a critical consciousness regarding the child's own language, thought, perception, and behavior because of the contrast between inclusive language and dominant cultural language. Children also can be encouraged to study other languages and cultures. In fact, such study would be most helpful, and perhaps should be required, if children are to develop critical consciousness. Children can be taught to be critical users of language as well as to develop inclusive language habits. However, the current social environment is so pervaded with sexism, including sexist language, that extra work is needed in the home, in the school, and in the faith congregation if sexist language is to be overcome. Unfortunately, these other sources frequently reinforce sexism.

Concluding Remarks

Linguistic habits, developed by societies over the centuries and by individuals within those societies over the course of a lifetime, are difficult to change. Whorfian thought indicates the influence that these linguistic habits can have upon individuals and societies. Despite the efforts of many linguists, analytic philosophers, and others, Whorf's principle of linguistic relativity survives and continues to encourage the possibility that critical consciousness, both individual and collective, can develop. Although traditional linguistic habits are difficult to alter, they can be. Better yet would be to develop a new tradition, a tradition of critical consciousness, a tradition that encourages the learning of multiple languages and cultures.

Chapter 5
Piaget's Genetic Epistemology and Language

In this chapter some of the work of Jean Piaget is explored in the context of issues of sexist language and inclusive language. Towards that goal, this chapter is organized as follows: (a) a description of genetic epistemology, including background information on Piaget, (b) a presentation of some assumptions and concepts central to genetic epistemology; (c) a description of Piaget's stages of cognitive development; (d) a presentation of language development within the context of genetic epistemology, (e) a discussion of some of the revisions of Piaget's original proposals, and (f) an application of Piagetian thought to the stubbornness of sexist language, to the possibilities of transformation to inclusive language, and to children growing up in a linguistically patriarchal society.

Genetic Epistemology

Jean Piaget selected the term "genetic epistemology" to describe his research. As the label suggests, Piaget studied the origins and development of cognition in human beings. Piaget believed that the basis for human cognition is to be found in the first physical movements that a child makes and then coordinates into sequences of movements (Piaget, 1971c, p. 140). From this simple foundation, Piaget traced the development of mathematical and scientific reasoning as that reasoning emerges in adolescence.

> Genetic epistemology attempts to explain knowledge, and in particular scientific knowledge, on the basis of its sociogenesis, and especially the psychological origins of the notions and operations upon which it is based. (Piaget, 1970, p. 1)

Genetic epistemology, as described by Piaget, is the study of the biological and psychological origins, as well as the development, of human cognition. In other words, Piaget studied and proposed a complex theory explaining how human beings acquire and maintain knowledge, going from lesser to greater states of cognition (Piaget, 1970, pp. 12-13).

Piaget also refers to himself as a "constructivist," one who believes that human beings play a significant role in the construction of their own knowledge. Piaget disagrees with both empiricism, as represented by John Locke, and innatism, as represented by Noam Chomsky. Piaget disagrees with empiricism because he does not believe that human beings are able to perceive reality directly, and because he does not believe that human beings acquire most or all of their knowledge from external experience (Piaget, 1977). Piaget disagrees with innatism because he does not believe that human beings are completely programmed with all the information needed for cognitive development (Piaget, 1977). Piaget believes that human beings actively participate in the acquisition and development of their own knowledge, integrating external data with internal structures.

A very important piece of background information regarding Piaget involves the relationship between biology and epistemology. Piaget earned his doctorate in zoology at Neuchatel, Switzerland in 1918 (Mays, 1972, pp. 305-306). That biological education was carried by Piaget throughout his research and writing. As is noted in the following subsection, Piaget incorporated into the foundation of his work the view that the biological principles apply to both the physical and the mental development of an organism, even a human organism.

Assumptions and Concepts

In this section some of the assumptions and concepts that are important in describing and understanding genetic epistemology are presented.

Assumptions

Piaget believed that the principles, concepts, and interactions that apply to biology also apply to cognition, and vice versa. "For Piaget, the one-time biologist, intelligence can be meaningfully considered only as an extension of certain fundamental biological characteristics, fundamental in the sense that they obtain wherever life obtains" (Flavell, 1963, p. 41). The connection between biology and cognition begins very early in the life of a human being. Piaget believed that the origins of knowledge could be traced to biological coordinations within the nervous system and the neural network (Piaget, 1970, p. 19), that intelligence begins with physical movements (Piaget & Inhelder, 1969, pp. 1-4), and that eventually thought can be regarded as action that has been interiorized (Flavell, 1963, p. 2).

The primary way in which the connection between biology and cognition expresses itself is in the two functional invariants that Piaget assumed: organization and adaptation. By functional invariant, Piaget means a process that is a biological, inherited way by which an organism interacts with its environment (Piaget & Inhelder, 1969, p. 7) and is a fundamental trait in the development of any life form.

> These invariant characteristics which define the essence of intellectual functioning and hence the essence of intelligence, are the very characteristics which hold for all biological functioning in general. All living matter adapts to its environment and possesses organizational properties which make the adaptation possible. (Flavell, 1963, p. 43)

Two other notions, also stemming from biology, that Piaget acquired early and retained were assimilation and equilibrium. Assimilation involves the ability of an organism to absorb information from outside of itself, altering that information so that it may be of use to the organism; "since every organism has a permanent structure, which can be modified under the influence of the environment but is never destroyed as a structured whole, all knowledge is always assimilation of a datum external to the subject's structure" (Piaget, 1971b, p. 8). Equilibrium involves the ability of an organism to attain some moments of rest or balance in, around, during, and between dealing with external data. Equilibrium applies to the mental and emotional aspects of an organism as much as it does to physical (biological) aspects. In the area of cognitive development, "the normative factors of thought correspond biologically to a necessity of equilibrium by self-regulation; thus, logic would in the subject correspond to a process of equilibrium" (Piaget, 1971b, p. 8).

In the following subsections, the concepts of organization, adaptation, assimilation and accommodation, and equilibrium are described from the perspective of genetic epistemology. The additional notions of equilibration, operations, cognitive egocentrism, and the semiotic function also are presented in the remaining subsections of this section.

Organization: Structure, Schema, and Stages (Periods)

All organisms arrange, or try to arrange, their experience so that the experience can be understood, internalized, and used in some way. This organization tendency applies to all organisms in dealing with all their realms of experience. For sentient creatures, such as human beings, this organization tendency includes the ways or patterns in which one thinks (Dreyer, 1984). This tendency to organization involves systems of relationships among the elements involved and an underlying coherence or pattern among those same elements (Flavell, 1963, pp. 44-52). In genetic epistemology, with its focus upon cognition, the organization tendency produces patterns of relationships that are intended to promote cognitive development. "Every act of intelligence presumes some kind of intellectual structure, some sort of organization, within which it proceeds" (Flavell, 1963, p. 46).

According to genetic epistemology, this capacity for organization results in what Piaget called structure. Structure involves the rules or guidelines of transformations (identity, reciprocity, and so on) and a system, such as mathematics, functioning in accordance with those rules (Piaget, 1970, pp. 22-23). Structure involves an organized system of mental actions. In order to expand the structure, the data presented for processing need to be on the edges of what the structure can handle; that is, optimal discrepancy is needed. Structures modify and are modified; they are not given preformed. Structures are constructed out of experience (Phillips, 1969, pp. 108-110). Structures also involve the reasons why a particular type of content is manifested; structures involve interpretation and expression of data (Flavell, 1963, p. 18).

The processing of experience by the structure occurs internally, within the organism, with the result that change occurs in the structure(s) or the substructure(s) involved; there are substructures as well as relationships between structures (Piaget, 1970, pp. 22-23). Structure involves the regular traits of an occurrence (Phillips, 1969, p. 7). Structures rarely, if ever, collapse completely, though they do undergo regular alteration as more data need to be dealt with—from eating to reading, from responding to a threat to explaining the latest astrophysical data. Structures "are the organizational properties of intelligence, organizations created through functioning and inferable from the behavioral contents whose nature they determine" as well as "mediators interposed between the invariant functions on the one hand and the variegated behavioral contents on the other" (Flavell, 1963, p. 17).

Structures begin developing before any of the higher cognitive functions emerge, yet structures are necessary for the development of those higher functions, including language. The most basic type of structure is called a scheme. "A scheme is a structure or organization of actions as they are transferred or generalized by repetition in similar or analogous circumstances" (Piaget & Inhelder, 1969, p. 4). Action schemes develop physically and externally in one situation and then their use is transferred to another situation. The earliest schemes, those of the infant, involve behavioral sequences such as sucking, grasping, looking. In the infant, these schemes are initially organic (instinctual and reflexive), then habits of actions develop during the sensori-motor period, and finally representational schemes emerge (Piaget, 1971a, pp. 181-182).

Schemes change constantly, via adaptation, seeking equilibrium; schemes are fluid structures which are built and then altered regularly as intellectual development proceeds (Flavell, 1963, p. 55). Schemes involve repeatable and generalizable coordinated actions and are the basis of logico-mathematical structures as some of these action schemes become interiorized (Piaget, 1970, p. 42). Further, certain kinds of structures develop prior to other kinds of structures. "Generally speaking, logico-mathematical structures are extracted from the general coordination of actions long before they make any use of language, either natural or artificial" (Piaget, 1971a, p. 181).

At certain points in the developmental process, qualitative shifts in the complexity of structures and schemes occur. Structures are thoroughly reorganized into more complex structures allowing additional ways of thinking, such as going from literal, concrete thinking to the ability to do counterfactual thinking. "Period" or "Stage" is the label used to denote these qualitative shifts in structures and schema (Flavell, 1963, p. 263).

Adaptation

Adaptation is the second functional invariant assumed by Piaget (Flavell, 1963, pp. 18-19) and is composed of two processes: assimilation and accommodation (Flavell, 1963, pp. 44-52; Dreyer, 1984), themselves presented in the next subsection. Adaptation occurs "whenever a given organism-environment interchange has the effect of modifying the organism in such a way that further interchanges, favorable to its preservation are enhanced" (Flavell, 1963, p. 45). Adaptation and organization, the other functional invariant, are interrelated; adaptation assumes the existence of some sort of organization while organizations are developed by means of adaptation (Flavell, 1963, p. 47).

Adaptation occurs at all levels of life. The mollusks that Piaget originally studied adapted to the water flow and temperatures of the streams in which they lived. The HIV adapts incredibly "well" and rapidly to its human hosts yet cannot adapt very well when outside the host; it lives for only a few seconds. Adaptation is involved in every exchange between the child and its environment, yet not every adaptation is successful. Failure to adapt can be due to inappropriate development for the experience involved or very unstable equilibrium or overwhelming of the structures involved by the experience or some combination of these factors. Higher level cognitive adaptation yields "much more complete results and much more stable structures" (Piaget, 1971a, p. 182). The concept of adaptation clearly can be traced to Piaget's study of zoology.

Assimilation and Accommodation

Assimilation and accommodation are the two processes of which adaptation is comprised. Descriptions of assimilation and accommodation within genetic epistemology tend to occur in pairs since the processes are so thoroughly intertwined. Assimilation involves an organism's dealing with environmental factors by making the data fit into the structures; accommodation involves the effort by an organism to fit its behavior to the environment. While both processes occur concurrently, one may be more dominant or visible at any given time (Donaldson, 1978, pp. 140-141). Assimilation and accommodation are two sides of the same coin.

"The filtering or modification of the input is called assimilation" (Piaget & Inhelder, 1969, p. 6). Assimilation refers to the process in which external stimuli or data are altered by the organism to fit existing structures; the first thing an organism does with an experience is to change the experience so that it is better understood (Dreyer, 1984). For example, in the study of a new subject, students often relate the new concepts or words to already known information; the new stimuli is assimilated into the knowledge patterns already possessed by the students. Not surprisingly, then, assimilation is a gradual, continuous process, since data that are completely outside the realm of experience of the subject cannot be incorporated because such experience would be unrelated to previous knowledge; totally new stimuli cannot be assimilated. An organism is able to assimilate only those items, events, or materials that the organism's past experience, including assimilations, enable it to incorporate (Flavell, 1963, p. 49). Assimilation then refers to the organism's altering its environment. This alteration is done so that elements in the environment can be more easily merged into the organization of the organism involved (Flavell, 1963, p. 45). Assimilation involves the altering of external data by processes or structures (Phillips, 1969, pp. 8-9) while at the same time structures are being preserved, or at least changed as little as possible (Donaldson, 1978, p. 141).

"Accommodation" refers to the process in which internal structures change to incorporate external stimuli. The internal patterns of dealing with external data are themselves altered in order to better use experience (Dreyer, 1984); "the modification of internal schemes to fit reality is called accommodation" (Piaget & Inhelder, 1969, p. 6). For example, in studying a new subject, students can stretch beyond their previous knowledge, altering their internal structures so that new data can be more easily understood, as opposed to the organism's making the data more familiar to itself (Flavell, 1963, p. 49). Accommodation also involves the organism's adjusting to the environment, as opposed to the organism's altering the environment as in assimilation (Flavell, 1963, p. 45). Accommodation describes modifications within the organism as well as increased opportunities for further change, for newness; "accommodation works for variability, growth, and change" (Donaldson, 1978, p. 141). While assimilation focuses on the altering of stimuli by the organism, accommodation involves the changing of the organism by the stimuli (Phillips, 1969, pp. 8-9).

The processes of assimilation and accommodation go together. Always, the organism is incorporating the environment (assimilation), the organism is adjusting to the environment (accommodation), and during both processes structures are being modified (Piaget, 1952, pp. 5-7). Data that are completely outside the structures or patterns of the organism cannot be assimilated into the organism nor can the organism accommodate itself to such data. "The mind can only be adapted to a reality if perfect accommodation exists" (Piaget, 1952, p. 7). Yet at the same time cognitive assimilation works to conserve the structures, thus minimizing change (Piaget, 1971a, p. 183).

Equilibrium

The goal of adaptation is described as equilibrium, the balancing of accommodation, assimilation, and structure (Donaldson, 1978, p. 141; Flavell, 1963, p. 239). However, while the goal may be moments of rest or balance, similar to a balanced scale, the goal is rarely achieved. In genetic epistemology, equilibrium describes "a state of continual activity, in which the organism compensates for—or cancels out—disturbances to the system, either actual or anticipated" (Donaldson, 1978, p. 140). Equilibrium is then, in part, the process of structures defining, weakening, and redefining themselves (Phillips, 1969, p. 10). Equilibrium involves a new balance, but rarely new by very much (Piaget, 1952, pp. 5-7). Further, achieving equilibrium is a very complex process.

> An internal mechanism . . . is observable at the time of each partial construction and each transition from one stage to the next. It is a process of equilibrium . . . in the sense . . . of self-regulation; that is, a series of active compensations on the part of the subject in response to external disturbances and an adjustment that is both retroactive (loop systems or feedbacks) and anticipatory, constituting a permanent system of compensations. (Piaget & Inhelder, 1969, p. 157)

Over time, equilibrium improves, with the organism's becoming able to handle more and more possibilities (Donaldson, 1978, pp. 155-156). The better the ability to handle more possibilities, the better the equilibrium. Equilibrium involves a harmony, or satisfactory pattern of interaction, with the environment (Donaldson, 1978, p. 140).

Equilibration

"Equilibration" is the name given by Piaget to describe the total functioning of the various processes. The equilibration process includes accommodation, assimilation, equilibrium, and organization. The process is initiated by an appropriate dissonance; if the dissonance is too great, then the organism is overwhelmed and shuts down or retreats; if the dissonance is too small, then the experience is easily incorporated and no change or growth occurs. The cognitive structures change to accept the dissonance (accommodation) or the structures incorporate the dissonance (assimilation) or some combination of the two processes occurs until a balance (equilibrium) is reached. Further, equilibrium reconciles maturation, social experience, and experience with objects (Piaget & Inhelder, 1969, pp. 158-159). "Thus, equilibrium by self-regulation constitutes the formative process of the structures we have described" (Piaget & Inhelder, 1969, p. 159).

Operations

Operations develop out of the physical actions of the infant as those actions gradually become internalized by the child who is growing and learning to do more activities through thinking. Eventually, operations are actions of great generality carried out in the mind, for example, combining, ordering, separating. The origins are in the Sensori-motor Period (Piaget, 1970, pp. 21-22). Operations are those actions that the child can imagine, that is, can eventually perform without benefit of physical movements, such as reversibility, addition and subtraction, negation, and soon; operations are always connected with other operations as part of systems and structures (Donaldson, 1978, p. 145).

> We . . . ,in studying the spontaneous development of scientific notions, have come to view as the central factor the very process of constructing operations, which consists in interiorized actions becoming reversible and coordinating themselves into patterns of structures subject to well-defined laws. (Piaget, 1962, p. 12)

Cognitive Egocentrism

In Piagetian thought, cognitive or epistemological egocentrism involves "the initial inability to decenter, to shift the given cognitive perspective" (Piaget, 1962, p. 3). That is, it involves "difficulty in understanding differences in points of view between the speakers and therefore in decentration" (Piaget & Inhelder, 1969, p. 118). The child understands or views the world, in all of its aspects, entirely from the child's perspective; the child is the center of the world. As the child grows and develops, the child becomes more able to see the world from other perspectives; such decentering involves a perpetual reformulation of previous points of view (Piaget, 1962, p. 3). Cognitive egocentrism "stems from a lack of differentiation between one's own point of view and the other possible ones" (Piaget, 1962, p. 4). As the child becomes more and more able to differentiate between differing perspectives, cognitive egocentrism lessens and decentration increases.

This inability to take the perspective of the other comes in various guises. For example, one type of cognitive egocentrism involves the child's perceiving the world as identical with the actions that the child makes—the world equals the child and the child's actions. In another type of cognitive egocentrism the representations of the world that the child makes are believed by the child to be the only representations possible; the child even can provide some degree of explanation for its own worldview but cannot comprehend that there are other perspectives. Still later another kind of cognitive egocentrism occurs when adolescents can imagine, without properly understanding, other possible perspectives but remain firmly convinced that their own worldview is the best, most accurate one, irrespective of the available evidence.

As the child grows, cognitive egocentrism changes in its effects. A nonoperational child is unable to explain why something happens the way it does, even when the child gets the right answer, and this lack of explanation is because the child is centered upon its own point of view. As decentration increases, as the child is able to see more and more from other perspectives, then the child's ability to explain also increases. Decreasing in cognitive egocentrism while increasing in decentration is important in learning reciprocal behaviors and in developing cooperation with others (Dreyer, 1984).

Semiotic Function

In Piagetian thought, the semiotic function is the capacity that, if allowed to develop, results in language. The semiotic function involves representing something by means of something else (Piaget & Inhelder, 1969, p. 5). The representation ranges from the relatively simple to the rather complex. For example, a word is often used to represent an object or an action; "dog" refers to a four-legged canine adored by many humans, and "walking" refers to a form of physical activity. "The Stars and Stripes," a complex symbol, has many meanings, and the conflict among these meanings often contributes to heated debates. The semiotic function expresses itself in various ways. The primary ways suggested by Piaget include language, gestures, deferred imitation, drawing, painting, and mental imagery, sometimes called internalized imitation (Piaget, 1970, p. 45). The semiotic function involves "the ability to represent something by a sign or a symbol or another object" (Piaget, 1970, p. 45).

Further, the development of the semiotic function is very much a part of the development of the child, and the bases for the development of the semiotic function are in the earliest physical movements of the child. Children whose physical development is delayed, that is whose reflexive schemes slowly develop, are more likely to have delayed development of the semiotic function as well. Blind and deaf children are delayed developmentally because their physical development is impaired; for them, the semiotic function does not develop as rapidly (Piaget, 1970, p. 46).

Cognitive Development

Since the development of language is part of and dependent upon cognitive development, a brief presentation of cognitive development according to Piaget is appropriate. In Piagetian thought, there are three periods, or stages, of cognitive development. These periods (with approximate ages) are as follows: the Sensori-motor Period (from birth to 18 months), the Concrete Operations Period (from 18 months to 11 years old) with two subperiods—a Pre-operations Subperiod (18 months to 7 years old) and a Concrete Operations Subperiod (7 years to

11 years), and the Formal Operations Period (11 years to 15 years).[1] Further, this developmental process involves complex interactions among four general factors: the experience of the child interacting with objects, the organic growth of the child, the social interaction of the child with other human beings, and the equilibration process (Piaget & Inhelder, 1969, pp. 152-159). Finally, this process is a biological, invariant course of cognitive development, that is, the periods always occur in the order given.

The Sensori-motor Period

The Sensori-motor Period is physical and the basis for all the development that ensues. The physical movements of the child become organized into reflexive schemes, such as looking and grasping. An infant's thinking is unreflective, very pragmatic in nature, and involves an imitative approach to life (Flavell, 1977, p. 56). The baby develops physical schemes in order to act upon the world. External data are assimilated into schemes and schemes change to accommodate the data; specifically, "assimilation to the child's own action prevails" (Piaget & Inhelder, 1969, p. 118). The child perceives the world as identical with the child's actions; the child is not able to take the perspective of the other.

Within the sensori-motor period, there are six phases involving primary, secondary, and tertiary circular reactions: exploring, seeking objects as ends, and using objects as means towards ends. Also in the sensori-motor period object-permanence develops. As the label suggests, the child begins to realize that objects do not cease to exist when the child is not perceiving them, that objects are, or tend to be, permanent. The infant is unable to make representations of objects in their absence until near the end of this period, in conjunction with the development of object-permanence. There is little overt language development in this period, and only indications of the semiotic function, but the foundations for language have been laid down.

The Concrete Operations Period

The pre-operations subperiod

In this subperiod the child can do things, get things done, but cannot explain why, though the child can make an effort to explain. This lack of real explanation is the reason both this subperiod and the sensori-motor period are considered non-operational by Piaget. The child in this period has a tendency to focus on one aspect of a situation or problem, as opposed to seeing the whole situation; the child's attention is limited and narrowly focused. The child is literal minded; in asking a child in this stage to do a particular task, one runs the risk that the child will do the task and nothing else that might normally be ex-

1. Detailed descriptions of Piaget's cognitive development periods are widely available. The sources for the following information, unless otherwise noted, are Flavell, 1977, pp. 14-91 & 99-118; Piaget & Inhelder, 1969, passim; & Dreyer, 1984.

pected. For example, the child may be asked to pick up the toys and may well pick up the toys most recently played with, leaving other toys and materials scattered and untouched. The child's attention is on the immediate situation: the toys being played with and the instructions being given. Deeper meanings and intentions are not noticed.

Some of the other traits of a child in this subperiod are as follows. The child has animistic ideas, such as that the sun is alive. The child does not understand equivalences, identities, functions and reversibility, but is noticing some of these relationships. Pre-operational children are egocentric in viewing reality from their own perspective and in believing that everyone else thinks as they do. Yet in this period the concept of object permanence is well established, the first real signs of representational thought appear, and this ability increases noticeably (Piaget, 1977). Accordingly, the semiotic function develops rapidly as seen in the increasing activity of the child in language usage, drawing, deferred imitation, and dance.

The concrete operations subperiod

Now the child is really beginning to develop. Inferences are much better. The child is able to focus on multiple aspects of a situation or problem, and soon will be able to focus on the whole picture. Objects can be, and quite often are, manipulated, intentionally and consciously, by the child. The transformations are known by the child to be reversible—inversion, reciprocity, conservation; transformations are more important than states. The child is able to explain accurately, though with difficulty, some of the transformations and the relationships involved therein; that is, the child can explain why the amount of water in the short, wide container is the same amount of water when poured into a taller, thinner container.

In this subperiod, representational abilities are much better as the child can do logical, propositional thinking. However, these abilities are still limited to tangible, concrete objects in the child's real, physical world of experience. The child cannot think about that which does not exist; counterfactuals cannot be consistently understood and maneuvered. The child remains focused on the concrete present, on a literal interpretation of what is said; hence the "letter of the law" attitude is characteristic of children in this stage: Following the rules is more important than some other ideal such as truth or justice or harmony. Further, the child still tends to be much more cognitively egocentric than decentered. The child's viewpoint is the perspective that dominates all other perspectives; the child's representations of the world of physical objects are the only possible representations (Phillips, 1969, p. 102). Yet the increase in representational abilities contributes to the further development of the semiotic function.

The Formal Operations Period

In the Formal Operations Period, the adolescent becomes liberated from the concrete, looks towards the future, and develops ideals. The transformations are understood and can be explained rather easily; most importantly, the adolescent understands and can explain the reversibility of the various transformations without the transformations being physically represented in front of the adolescent. Formal operational thinkers can perform introspection; that is, they can think about thought.

Counterfactual reasoning is possible; hypothetical reasoning and the deduction of consequences can be done independently of the actual truth or falsity of the premises (Piaget, 1972, pp. 2-3). Abstract reasoning and alternatives to the present reality can be considered. Hypotheses can be, and are, developed and tested; hypothetical-deductive reasoning involves orderly, syllogistic-style thinking, formal logic, and the development of the scientific method. Formal operational persons can imagine the possibilities, then verify or disprove the various possibilities via the systematic exploration of those possibilities and their possible combinations.

In this period decentration is more developed as more variables are considered: the self, the self's behavior, others, the world, and so on. Also, cognitive egocentrism involves the adolescent's new capacities as thinking extends into the hypothetical-deductive realm; adolescents can see other perspectives but tend to believe that their perspectives are the ideal ones (Phillips, 1969, p. 102).

Language Development

As suggested in the preceding section, language development in human beings occurs in conjunction with the development of the semiotic function and is based upon the development of action schemes that begin in infancy. As schemes develop, they become more complex, reorganizing themselves as data are assimilated and accommodated. The sensori-motor schemes are patterns of behavior that are based in, and develop out of, physical activity. Further, the semiotic function is based upon schemes or structures that involve patterns of representational behavior. These patterns are evolving and becoming more complex as the child develops. Structures incorporate and rearrange material, resulting in newly modified structures or patterns of organization.

In Piagetian thought, language is one strand in the web known as the semiotic function; other strands include symbolic play, deferred imitation, drawing, and mental images. All of these strands involve the child's ability to represent some event or person or place or thing or action by means of some other event or person or place or thing or action. Object permanence is important in the development of the semiotic function; one needs to realize that the signified, or the referent, is permanent in order to be able to represent it (Flavell, 1977, pp. 40-49).

Language is not identical with thought but language enhances thought; delays in linguistic development result in delays in thought development, as studies with deaf and blind children show (Piaget & Inhelder, 1969, pp. 84-90). As language develops, it comes to exercise greater and greater influence upon the continued development of symbolic representation. Language enhances not only thought but also human communication with others (Piaget & Inhelder, 1969, pp. 56-57). Language assists humans in reducing cognitive egocentrism and in increasing decentration. "Language is the vehicle par excellence of symbolization, without which thought could never become really socialized and thereby logical" (Flavell, 1963, p. 155).

The development of language depends upon the quality of the development of numerous other factors. These factors include infant reflexive schemes, equilibration, object permanence, the interiorization of thought, decreasing cognitive egocentrism, increasing decentration, and the semiotic function. Language is neither completely learned nor completely preprogrammed but is rather the ongoing result of a complex set of factors.

Revisions

Piaget's research has been revised by followers as well as by Piaget himself (Piaget, 1972; Piaget, 1977). The periods remain invariant. However, the rate of progress through the stages varies much more widely than Piaget initially believed, sometimes due to genetic factors, sometimes due to environmental factors, and sometimes due to a combination of these factors. For example, children who are deaf or blind go through the stages more slowly than physically healthy children; urban children from Tehran proceed more rapidly through the stages than do children from the Iranian mountains (Piaget, 1977).

Also, the rate of progress can vary due to the interest of the children in the materials being used; that is, a curiosity or interest or experience factor is involved. A child tested with unfamiliar materials would seem "slower" than a child tested with familiar materials. For example, using tinker toys with children who have never seen or used anything like tinker toys will result in those children being viewed as less developed than they otherwise might have been. "Thus, although formal operations are logically independent of the reality content to which they are applied, it is best to test the young person in a field which is relevant to [that person's] career and interests" (Piaget, 1972, p. 1). Since persons can vary in cognitive development depending upon areas of interest and familiarity, stages can vary with the activity or topic (Piaget, 1972). A person may function in formal operations in some areas and in concrete operations in other areas.

Structure and Content (Data)

Piaget often suggests that content is independent of structure, and this independence is clearest in the Formal Operations Period when a person has learned to think about possibilities without being limited by the concrete. Yet in his 1972 article in *Human Development* Piaget acknowledges the connection between content and structure in his recognition that a young person's interest in and experience with a subject will assist that young person in advancing through the stages with respect to that subject area. In other words, advancing through the cognitive stages is related to content. Accordingly, if one lacks interest, then one will advance more slowly, if at all. If a person can be at different stages depending upon the subject, then one can be formal operational in dealing with automobiles while still in concrete operations when it comes to sex-roles.

In response to Piaget's emphasis on distinguishing between structure and data is Piaget's own theory of development, in which the process begins in sensori-motor behavior. Structures emerge as patterns of organizing physical actions. If the structures are viewed as being distinct from behavior and content, then Piaget may be committing the fallacy of misplaced concreteness. That is, the patterns into which data have been and are being organized are taken to be real apart from their involvement with the data. Yet, as Piaget says, when the structures assimilate and accommodate to data, the structures are modified and content is incorporated into reorganized structures.

Cognitive Egocentrism

Donaldson (1978, pp. 10-11, 19-25, 55-56) claims that children are not as egocentric as Piaget believes them to be; their apparent egocentrism involves a variety of factors in communication, in the children's dependency on nonverbal clues, and in working with materials that may or may not be familiar to the children. Donaldson shows that, if the situation is familiar and the materials and tasks understood, egocentrism in young children is not as extreme as Piaget believed. A child "first makes sense of situations . . . and then uses *this* kind of understanding to help" in responding to what is being asked (Donaldson, 1978, pp. 56). At least three factors are involved in a child's response to tasks: (a) the child's knowledge of the language, (b) the child's assessment of what we intend based upon non-linguistic factors, and (c) the way in which the child would interpret the physical situation for themselves if the adults were not present (Donaldson, 1978, p. 68). Language in and for itself is difficult enough for a child to grasp. When testing situations are involved the situation becomes even more tricky. Accordingly, then, for the child, non-linguistic clues are very important (Donaldson, 1978, p. 69). When a child is able to use familiar materials and to cue in on the appropriate nonverbal signals, then decentration is more apparent, and cognitive egocentrism is lessened.

Applications of Genetic Epistemology

Stubbornness

According to genetic epistemology, children begin learning in the sensori-motor period, and this learning continues through the concrete operations period. Young children incorporate much data before they begin speaking. And before children begin speaking, they have begun to understand and communicate. Given the developmental processes and factors described by Piaget, if sexism enters into the developmental process early, then the sexist data are more likely to be carried along in the various reorganizations of structure and data that occur. In U.S. cultures, sexism communicated by means of images, tone of voice, feelings, and understanding as in nonverbal cuing, does enter the developmental process at a prelinguistic level. For example, the image of "God the Father" is acquired very early. As Piaget and others have noted, assimilation is a conservative process, the data that enter a person's experience early are most difficult to alter.

Language emerges as a very important factor in the cognitive developmental process. If the child's stimuli, from language and other sources, remain sexist, then the cognitive processes will be more likely to remain sexist. Since sexism and sexist language are quite common, the sexist data continue to be integrated into modified structures, adding to the sexism already present, unless ongoing conscious efforts are made to exclude the sexist material. Once acquired, language becomes a powerful influence upon the continued development of symbolic representation. Even if a child has had no pre-linguistic sexist experiences, sexist language from external sources would begin to exercise great influence once language sufficiently develops.

In concrete thought, a word literally is identical with the concept or event or object being named. For example, to a formal operations thinker in the study of religion, "God the Father" would probably not be construed literally as a male deity. However, to a concrete operations thinker, "God the Father" is literally a powerful male figure, especially given the tradition and repetition reinforcing that image. On the other hand, to a formal operations thinker, "God the Mother" should be equally unproblematic. Yet to a concrete operations thinker, the image of "God the Mother" probably is too dissonant to be assimilated because such an image would be beyond the range of images that has been embedded in the cognitive structures. Concrete thinkers tend to be stuck in a realm of literal experience.

Given the developmental processes involved—adaptation, equilibration, and so on—content and structure are important; both help convey meaning. If language is sexist, then the behavior and the internal structures must be influenced in sexist ways because language develops out of behavior. And once language emerges out of the semiotic function, it in turn becomes a powerful influence, providing even more stimuli. If the new linguistic data are sexist, then the probability of sexism's continuing increases.

Transformation

From genetic epistemology two foundations for transforming from sexist language to inclusive language can be noted. One basis can be found in altering the initial data—those first images, voice tones, and so on—that an infant encounters. If the data taken into the early development of structures are inclusive, then the probability of inclusive language developing will increase. Using inclusive language and behavior from the very beginning of a child's life provides one foundation for transformation.

The other basis is to utilize the equilibration process. Small bits of dissonance, administered appropriately, can serve to adjust the structures to the point where inclusive language becomes part of the structure. While it is possible that a radical dissonance can trigger a radical "breakthrough" experience in some persons, such experiences would seem to be minimal. If equilibrium with respect to sexism and sexist language is not disturbed, sexism and sexist language will become more and more entrenched. A constant, but not overwhelming, disruption of the equilibrium will get results, depending upon the context. Too much dissonance can easily result in the person turning off or reverting to an earlier more comfortable, and probably more sexist, level of development.

Since language, once it begins to develop, becomes a very important factor in cognitive development, utilizing an inclusive language would begin a process of developing cognitive structures with less and less sexism in them. New mental structures can be liberating from the past and inaugurating of new activities towards the future (Piaget & Inhelder, 1969, p. 151).

The Story

Applying Piagetian thought to the paradigmatic story introduced at the beginning of this study yields the following two results. First, girls seem more able to decenter than boys. The girls were able to imagine what they would do if they were boys as indicated by the girls actually identifying new vocational choices. Some boys apparently could decenter, could see the perspective of being a girl, did not like what they "saw," and would rather be "nothing" or "dead" than be a girl. Most of the boys apparently could not decenter, since they could not respond to the question.

Also, both the girls and the boys have adapted to societal expectations as indicated by their vocational choices to both questions. In response to the question, "What do you want to be when you grow up?", the girls choose traditional female occupations just as the boys choose traditional male occupations in response to the first question. In response to the second question, pretending to be the opposite sex now "What do you want to be?", the girls were able to select traditional male vocations. In this situation, the boys were either unable to participate or unwilling to consider the possibilities of being a girl in a patriarchal society. Those boys who can consider the possibility of being girls do not like that possibility; they have *adapted* all too well.

Concluding Remarks

Piaget's research focused on the origins and development of human knowledge, beginning with the child's first physical movements and continuing with the study of how one structure changes into another structure. Piaget discovered an invariant sequence of structures, though further research has altered the original timetable and the scope of the process. Initially Piaget believed that a child either was completely in a particular Stage or Period in all of its mental activities or not in that particular period. Later Piaget came to believe that a child's familiarity with the materials being used and interest in the topics being discussed did affect the child's development. That is to say, children can move through the stages at varying speeds depending upon environmental and physical factors; also a child can move at varying speeds through different topics. Accordingly, a child can be formal operations in all or most areas, or formal operations in some areas but not all. What remains constant is the impact that the early experiences have on the child; once data get into the system, such data are difficult to remove.

Structures deal with data, otherwise the structures would be organizing nothing, operating on air. Data upset the equilibrium of the organism, thereby triggering the equilibration process. So, content is involved in the developmental process. If the data are sexist, as in the case of the linguistic environment into which children are born and within which children are raised, then the children will integrate sexism into their cognitive structures. Sexism will be part of the very fabric of their thought and language, as is demonstrated in the paradigmatic story of the children that opens this study. Providing inclusive data—images, language, and so on—in lieu of sexist language data, is one way of beginning to transform society from patriarchy to inclusivity, although providing an inclusive environment would seem quite improbable in today's society. For those of us with sexist structures already well-developed, the means of change involve providing appropriate dissonance, such as inclusive or nonsexist language, that upsets our equilibrium and encourages us to develop a critical awareness of our use of language.

Chapter 6
A Summary of Insights
from Whitehead, Whorf and Piaget

The tripartite thesis of this study is (a) that language shapes how human beings perceive reality, (b) that the development of theoretical constructs can help explain resistances to and possibilities for inclusive language, and (c) that the implementation of inclusive language is an important goal for religious education. The goal in this chapter is to demonstrate that the results of the explorations conducted in Chapters 3, 4, and 5 support the claims that language shapes how human beings perceive reality and that the development of theoretical constructs can help explain resistances to and possibilities for inclusive language.[1] Towards fulfilling the goal, this chapter is organized as follows: (a) a discussion of the role of language in shaping perception, in light of the work of Whitehead, Whorf, and Piaget; (b) a presentation of theoretical constructs from the work of Whitehead, Whorf, and Piaget as they help explain resistances to and possibilities for inclusive language; (c) a discussion of the paradigmatic story that opens this study from the perspectives of Whitehead, Whorf, and Piaget; and (d) concluding remarks.

Language and the Perception of Reality

All three perspectives presented in this study support the first subthesis, that language shapes how human beings perceive reality. Of the three perspectives used in this study, Whorf's linguistic relativity is the clearest in its support of the first subthesis. In fact, most of the intense debate about Whorfian thought involves exactly this point—the degree to which language affects human perception, thought, and behavior. Those thinkers who most fervently reject linguistic relativity believe that the shaping of human perception of reality by language is minimal, if real at all. Even among those thinkers who accept some form of linguistic relativity, there is debate over the degree to which language affects human perception of reality. Given the interpretation of linguistic relativity presented in Chapter 4, human language shapes human perception of reality to the degree that the language is unconsciously accepted, used, and perpetuated. Further, sexist linguistic habits contribute to both perception and behavior, which themselves then tend to be sexist. From the perspective of Whorfian thought, language shapes how human beings perceive reality.

Whitehead's philosophy of organism provides more obvious support for the first subthesis than does Piaget's genetic epistemology but less obvious support than does Whorf's principle of linguistic relativity. The results of the exploration in Chapter 3 of Whiteheadian thought indicate that language is one of the factors that does shape how human beings perceive and interpret the events and

---

1. The third part of the thesis, the aspect dealing with the implementation of inclusive language as an important goal for religious education, is discussed in Chapter 7.

patterns of events which constitute reality. An additional result is that the more sexist the linguistic world of a person is, the more likely it is that the person's perception of social reality is also sexist. There are, of course, factors that influence language, factors such as thought and behavior; in a philosophy of organism, influence is multidirectional. Within Whiteheadian thought, while human language does not unilaterally control human perception of reality, human language is nevertheless a very important factor in shaping how human beings perceive reality.

Of the perspectives used in this study, genetic epistemology is least obvious in its support of the first subthesis. However, support is available. Structures affect perception, with sensorimotor activities providing the foundation for all the development that follows, including cognitive and semiotic development. These structures are influenced by language. Language affects perception, then, by means of the incorporation of linguistic content into the structures upon which the equilibration process works. For example, language encourages a worldview in which "things," not processes, are the basic units, and such a worldview develops in children around the age of 10 years old (Fetz, 1988, pp. 268-271). At the age of 10 the child is in the Concrete Operations Period, with a very literal outlook, and language has had enough time to do its work. Since the type of language used affects the perception of reality, a constantly used sexist language contributes to a sexist perception of reality. According to the presentation in Chapter 5, genetic epistemology supports the claim that language shapes how human beings perceive reality.

The Development of Theoretical Constructs

Theoretical constructs can be used to explain both the resistance to inclusive language and the possibilities for inclusive language; such constructs have been presented in the preceding chapters. The resistance to inclusive language has been discussed in conjunction with the stubbornness of sexist language. The possibilities for inclusive language have been discussed in conjunction with the possibilities for transformation to inclusive language. The resistance of sexist language can be explained, not explained away, using Whiteheadian thought or Whorfian thought or Piagetian thought or some combination of these perspectives. Likewise, within each of these perspectives are some bases for hope, that is, some conceptual possibilities for encouraging inclusive language.

Philosophy of Organism

From the viewpoint of the philosophy of organism, resistance to inclusive language is closely connected with the stubbornness of sexist language, and sexist language is truly persistent. Sexist language has long been dominant in the English-language tradition; sexist linguistic habits are deeply embedded in the metaphysical process. Sexist language events are much more prevalent in the initial data, including propositions, than are inclusive-language events, and thereby are more likely to be selected by language-using creatures. The power of the past, especially of repetition, increase the stubbornness of sexist language and thereby also increase the resistance to inclusive language. For humans these factors work on unconscious as well as conscious levels. If the data are predominantly sexist, then language is likely to be sexist; also the accompanying thought, perception, and behavior are more likely to be sexist, since these aspects are interrelated.

Within a philosophy of organism, possibilities for transforming to inclusive language can be based upon the freedom of creatures and the lure of the Divine. Choices are made from among possibilities, and each creature has some degree of freedom; human beings especially have more self-determination than other creatures. Within the initial data and propositions, there are elements or strands of inclusive language that are available for selection by individuals. Individuals can, given self-determination and some inclusive-language data, cultivate a habit of inclusive language that would replace their sexist language habit. Developing a habit of inclusive language may take many starts. Also, selection from the initial data can be guided by the lure of the Divine towards inclusiveness, including inclusive language. If the lure of the Divine is towards inclusiveness, including inclusive language, then choices towards exclusiveness, including sexist language, are a form of ignoring the Divine and of perpetuating patriarchal power. The philosophy of organism provides explanations for both the persistence of sexist language and the possibility of an emerging inclusive language.

Linguistic Relativity

Whorf's linguistic relativity clearly indicates the connections between language, thought, perception, and behavior. The implication is that sexist language will contribute to sexist thought, sexist perceptions, and sexist behavior. From the perspective of Whorfian thought, the use of sexist language has a powerful influence on the thought, perception, and behavior of the individual. Further, the stronger the influence, the more unaware a person is of that influence. With this lack of critical consciousness comes an acceptance of "natural logic" or "common sense" regarding language. Finally, insofar as language is treated as background phenomenon, this treatment contributes to deeply embedded linguistic habits.

The primary basis for inclusive language involves developing critical consciousness regarding linguistic usage. Developing a critical self-awareness of one's linguistic habits can assist a person in using more appropriate language, including inclusive language. Critical consciousness can be developed in both adults and children. Adults can learn, although expanding horizons beyond one's linguistic tradition can be difficult. While Whorf never applied his own insights to sexist language, his appreciation for Native American languages demonstrates that adults can go beyond their linguistic traditions. Introducing inclusive language early and comprehensively would help children develop habits of inclusive language. New languages can be learned; children need not be linguistically stifled. Further, changing the language can help alter a person's thought, perception, and behavior. Sexist linguistic habits can be changed into habits of inclusive language, and such change will contribute towards inclusive practice.

Whorfian thought can help to explain both resistance to and possibilities for inclusive language and therefore supports both parts of the second subthesis.

Genetic Epistemology

Piagetian thought can help to illuminate the pervasive stubbornness of sexist language by pointing to the lack of early experience in inclusive language, the concrete nature of thought that is not escaped, and the lack of appropriate dissonance in the course of development. From a Piagetian perspective, when sexist language is part of the ongoing cognitive development of a child, then the child is more likely to organize interpretive schemes that contain sexist data as part of the structure, thereby influencing the child's view of the world. The child's ongoing equilibration process will be continually influenced by the sexist elements of the structures; that is, sexist language is adapted into the patterns of behavior and neural functioning early in a child's life, and what is impressed early is hard to eliminate: Assimilation is a conservative process.

Given the quantity of sexist language encountered in the United States of America, it is not surprising that patriarchal standards are accepted too easily by those persons who remain somewhere within the Concrete Operations Period. People who remain in the Concrete Operations Period tend to take what is said literally and have difficulty in dealing with meanings intended beyond a literal interpretation of words involved. Further, if accommodation is to be successful, dissonance needs to be appropriate to the person as well as appropriate to the circumstances. If the dissonance is too great, then the organism is likely to shut down, not see, or in some way ignore the data; if the dissonance is too little, then the change in the structures is minimal.

One basis for transformation would be in altering the data for all persons, but especially for young children; data include tone of voice, images, phrases, words, and more, so that the developing structures can incorporate inclusive as opposed to sexist data. The other basis for inclusive language involves the appropriate use of dissonance. For adults especially, small bits of dissonance such as modeling, stories, examples, and personal experiences can be used to encourage decentering and counterfactual thinking. Increasing experience and appropriate dissonance can aid the transformation to inclusive language and reduce sexist language. The use of appropriate inclusive language will influence the content to which the structures adapt, thereby moving the structures towards more inclusivity. The more the structures and the content are influenced by inclusive language, the more likely that perception, thought, and behavior also will be inclusive. Theoretical constructs from genetic epistemology can help to explain both resistance to and possibilities for inclusive language.

The Story

Within a Whiteheadian perspective, most children have been strongly influenced by the power of the past, and that past contains far greater amounts of sexist data, including sexist language, than of inclusive data. Further, the sexist data are much more easily accessible than are the inclusive data. Using inclusive language is very nontraditional and therefore unlikely to be imagined by children raised and socialized in a sexist milieu. In the representative story that opens this study, the girls seem more willing to participate than do the boys in that the girls respond to the question of what they would like to be if they were boys. The girls also appear to be more aware of other possibilities, even within the patriarchal culture of which they are products. Even so, both the girls and the boys are clearly products of their culture. With increasing use of inclusive language, the possibilities for children to be able to participate in the exercise and not change their vocational choices based upon sex also would increase.

Within the perspective of Whorfian thought, the children have been raised in a society in which the linguistic habits have, for the most part, encouraged male human beings and discouraged female human beings. Young children re-pattern and are otherwise creative with language, but in the socialization process creativity is suppressed; conformity is strongly encouraged and rewarded. Children come to participate fully in the dominant language of the culture. Children come to accept language as a background phenomenon as well as to accept the view of natural logic or commonsense toward language—namely, that anyone who speaks a language fluently is an expert user of that language. In the narrative when the girls choose traditionally male vocations which have high public esteem, this indicates that most of the girls recognize, at least unconsciously, the situation in which they find themselves. Likewise, when some of the boys would rather be "dead" or "nothing" than be a girl, this indicates that some of the boys, at least unconsciously, recognize the patriarchal situation in which they are located. Since children are not encouraged to develop a critical awareness regarding language, children are controlled by the language.

Within the perspective of Piagetian thought, the children in the story have adapted all too well to societal expectations, as is indicated in their responses to the initial question—"What do you want to be when you grow up?" This adaptation represents what happens to children all too frequently. However, the dissonance introduced by the request to pretend to be the opposite sex and then to respond to the same question seems to be accommodated by the girls better than by the boys, given the levels of response. The girls may well be able to handle this dissonance because they have experienced a similar dissonance in the conflict between their own feelings, thoughts, and hopes and the views dominant in society. This previous experience of dissonance would then contribute to the overall cognitive development of the girls, as well as to the ability of the girls to decenter and to use counterfactual thinking. Both their ability to decenter and to use counterfactual thinking are indicated in the girls' willingness to participate in their exercise.

The lack of dissonance between their own experience and societal expectations would appear to contribute to the unwillingness of most of the boys to participate in the reversal exercise. This unwillingness to participate indicates an inability to decenter or to use counterfactual thinking. The children are functioning in the Concrete Operations Period, with the adaptation being such that the boys tend to be slightly more literal and the girls tend to be slightly more aware of other perspectives.

Children see, hear, feel and otherwise receive information from television, family, peers, adults, parents, and many other sources. The vast majority of that information—the words, pictures, images, feelings, attitudes, tones, and so on— promotes and confirms the stereotypes, that boys become doctors, girls become nurses, and all the rest. These stereotypes are learned by children beginning very early in their lives. Even in families where inclusivity and equality are promoted, the non-home sources are so overwhelming, especially the mass media, that sexism is implanted and reinforced; this early imprinting can be altered but effort is needed to do so.

With respect to sexist language and inclusive language, speakers of English and similar languages are in the habit of using sexist language, such as the pseudo-generics "he" and "man," and these are used either alone or in conjunction with other words, such as mankind or mailman. Children hear, see, feel, and imitate, and another habit is established—a habit of linguistic sexism. Lamb suggests that the brain develops neural pathways that change and can be changed over time (Lamb as cited in Regan, 1988b, p. 8); perhaps, then, sexist pathways can be weakened and inclusive language pathways strengthened. The repetition of patriarchal language serves to perpetuate societal norms, even possible careers. Usually girls are not encouraged to consider all the possibilities, nor are boys. Girls are discouraged from some pursuits, such as science, and encouraged in others, such as nursing. Likewise boys are encouraged in some vocations, such as engineering, and discouraged from others, such as child care. The society-wide implementation of truly inclusive language would contribute to the development of a more inclusive society.

Concluding Remarks

The perspectives of Whitehead, Whorf, and Piaget support the first two parts of the thesis of this study, namely that language shapes human perception of reality and that theoretical constructs can help to explain both resistances to and possibilities for inclusive language. All three thinkers put emphasis on pre-linguistic experience as the basis of thought; all three suggest that, once language develops, it comes to have a significant influence on thought. Further, thought influences perception and behavior in all three systems, and language influences perception and behavior. The influence of language on thought, perception, and behavior is not, of course, unilateral; all of these factors are mutually influential. Finally, in all three systems linguistic habits are difficult to alter, but these habits can be altered; transformation is possible. Given the presentations of Whiteheadian, Whorfian, and Piagetian thought the first two parts of the tripartite thesis of this study have been supported.

The views of Whitehead, Whorf, and Piaget are compatible with each other. A common emphasis on process, instead of an emphasis on substance, encourages the compatibility. The philosophy of organism can be viewed as providing the overarching metaphysical framework within which linguistic relativity and genetic epistemology demonstrate more specific and quite appropriate applications of a process perspective. A point-by-point correspondence is not being claimed, but there appear to be significant overlaps, and the differences seem to complement each other. While a more thorough integration of these three views is beyond the scope of this study, the material so far presented gives some indication of possible agreements among genetic epistemology, linguistic relativity, and the philosophy of organism.[2]

2 A synthesis of a Whiteheadian philosophy of organism, a Whorfian linguistic relativity, and a Piagetian genetic epistemology into a still more comprehensive paradigm has not been done, though there are some works in which the comparing, contrasting, and integrating of two of the three schools of thought has begun. Some connections between Whorf and Whitehead have been explored in Olewiler (1971) and in Regan (1982). Connections between Piaget and Whorf have been explored in Bloom (1981). An initial comparison of the ontologies of Whitehead and Piaget has been made by Fetz (1988). Probably the most extensive integration of Whitehead and Piaget has occurred in The Anisa Model. The Anisa Model is an attempt to provide a comprehensive educational system, with Whiteheadian thought and Piagetian thought providing the conceptual framework. For a sampling of The Anisa Model, see Jordan (1974), Jordan & Shepard (1972), Jordan & Streets (1973), Kalinowski & Jordan (1973), Raman (1975), and Streets & Jordan (1973).

Chapter 7
The Importance of Inclusive Language
for Religious Education

Whether "the implementation of inclusive language is an important goal for religious education" (the third subthesis of this study) depends upon multiple factors. Among these factors are the influence language is believed to exert on thought, perception, and behavior; the description of religious education being considered; how the relationship between religious education and theology is construed; and the view held of the relationship between patriarchy and the religious institution involved. Chapters 3, 4, 5, and 6 of this study demonstrate the important role that language plays in human life, given the perspectives of Whitehead, Whorf, and Piaget. In considering the third subthesis, this chapter contains sections on the description of religious education used in this study and its relationship to theology, patriarchy, and the Christian church, a case for inclusive language within Christianity, and a direct discussion of whether or not "the implementation of inclusive language is an important goal for religious education."[1]

Religious Education and Theology

According to the description of religious education presented in Chapter 2 of this study, a description based largely upon Whitehead's philosophy of education, religious education involves helping people find ways to live with integrity, ways that maintain and encourage healthy lives and relationships, and to overcome the isolation and selfishness that are moving the human species towards extinction. Duty and reverence, as referred to by Whitehead, reflect concern for the obligation of human beings to learn, to exercise that learning as appropriately as possible throughout daily living, and to realize that every moment is sacred and in some way connected with every other moment. The present emerges out of the past, and the future arises out of the present. In addition to being inclusive, this view of religious education is comprehensive. That is, all true education is religious education. Further,

> [A] genuinely religious education will be one that rages against all separation, division and injustice. It will also be one that includes the voices of persons

---

1. Religious education in general is the main focus of this study. Most of the examples used come from Christianity because I am most familiar with that tradition. However, neither theology nor religious education should be construed as involving only Christianity. Inclusive language is threatening to patriarchal theology wherever that type of theology is found.

everywhere in attempting the educational work of interpreting the totality of human reality and experience. (Withers, 1985, p. 652)[2]

The relationship between religious education and theology can be construed in different ways. Traditionally, religious education has been considered the servant of theology. Theology discussed and decided what was important; the job of religious education was to convey, by appropriate means, the decisions of theology to the laity. Alternatively, the relationship between religious education and theology implied in this study is more complex than the traditional view. The interconnectedness among language, thought, perception, and behavior indicated in this study gives rise to an interactive view of the relationship between religious education and theology. Developments and discussions occurring in religious education have an effect upon developments and discussions occurring in theology. The influence of religious education upon theology can range from the very minimal and not very obvious to the more influential and more overt. The complex interplay among language, thought, behavior, and perception, as indicated in Chapters 3, 4, 5, and 6, suggests that developments in religious education do feed back into and influence theology.

The perspectives discussed in this study indicate the influence that language has on many other aspects of life and how this influence can ripple throughout various arenas of human endeavor. An intentionally patriarchal theology, be it conscious or unconscious, is reinforced by, and reinforces, sexist language. Likewise, an inclusive theology is reinforced by and reinforces inclusive language. Discrepancies between a theology and the language used in dis-

---

2 .   One criticism of feminist theology is that it is too white, too limited in the socioeconomic experience from which it draws and to which it appeals, and too Western. One result of this narrowness is that issues of race, ethnicity, and socioeconomic status (class) are too often ignored. Examples of this criticism can be found in Grant (1989), Pui-lan (1985), and Williams (1985 & 1986). Grant (1989) provides a comprehensive discussion of the narrowness of Feminist theology and states that Feminist theology is both too white and racist (Grant, 1989, p. 199). Accordingly, Grant suggests that women of color should refer to themselves "womanists" (as described by Alice Walker) instead of feminists (Grant, 1989, p. 203). Grant also believes that a wholistic theology would best begin with a complex analysis of black women's experience because their experience involves race, sex, and class issues (Grant, 1989, p. 198). Grant also challenges womanist theology to deal with the sexism in traditional language. Beginnings have been made to deal with the aforementioned critique as, for example, in Brock (1992), Pui-lan (1983 & 1984) and Russell, Pui-lan, Isasi-Diaz, & Cannon (1988). For a non-theological discussion of the issues of race, sex, and class see Weis (1988).

As indicated in Chapter 1 (p. 22), addressing these important concerns is beyond the scope of this study. However, the approach to inclusive language taken in this study is intended to support such an effort. Inclusive language would support developing an inclusive theology. Paying attention to all the ways in which language is used to oppress and deceive is part of the view of inclusive language used in this study. Further, seriously accounting for all experience, especially the experience of "the least of these" is part of the Whiteheadian spirit of this study.

cussing that theology can lead to problems, such as some persons being left out or a perspective being undermined. The importance or lack of importance, of inclusive language for religious education varies from individual to individual or from group to group. Inclusive language, given the perspectives of Whitehead, Whorf, and Piaget, is an important factor in promoting other types of inclusivity.

Patriarchy and the Church

One of the contexts in which patriarchy is involved is with the Christian Church. The patriarchal view of men as superior to all other beings has been, and still is, reinforced by the God-the-Father language that dominates most church settings today (Gray, 1982, p. 72). Many, perhaps most, church members indicate that for them God is beyond male and female, yet the words most used to describe God are male terms which also put God at the top of a pyramid of power (Withers, 1980, p. 82).

> Nowhere is woman's experience of male-dominated language more pervasive than in the church and synagogue. Such 'he' language is applied 'in the generic sense' to God, to the preacher, to the worshiper. In hymns, liturgies, and styles of government, religious life is male-oriented. It is *generic nonsense* to say that women are included linguistically when they are excluded by so many practices. (Russell, 1974, p. 95)

That God is really conceived of as male can be seen in other ways as well. Try asking yourself or the people around you or your students if you are involved in a teaching situation to replace the term God with the term Goddess for merely 30 days; note the reactions and then note how many actually attempt the task. One author reviewed 328 hymns requested on a British Broadcasting Corporation show and found the single most frequent image to be a male god with power over others; no female nouns or pronouns were found in any of the hymns, and only a few neutral pronouns were found (Wren, 1989, pp. 115-122). Of course the incorporating of patriarchy begins early in life.

> Even a small child on the street who couldn't care less about a transcendental being will say any time, 'Of course God is a man. He has a beard, hasn't he?' And the male child, as a man, and the male-identified woman unconsciously identify with the male rulership of the world. (Morton, 1985, p. 180)

Resistance to using inclusive language occurs in the Christian Church and is a clear indication that discussions over language are not just debates about "mere words." "If few people believe the Divine is sexed however, whence the resistance to words that alternatively describe God/ess as female and male, He and She?" (Smith, 1985, p. 635). If people really believe that the Divine is beyond sex, then there should be no debate over using female terms and feminine imagery for the Divine, assuming those terms and that imagery to be Biblically based. Since the debate continues, many, perhaps most, Christians really do believe, perhaps unconsciously, that the Divine is male. "The resistance to changing male God language would indicate (even in the face of violent denial) that *the male God is meant"* (Morton, 1985, p. 150).

Joanmarie Smith suggests that the responses of the boys to the question of what they would like to be when they grow up if they were girls (in the paradigmatic story that opens this study) is strongly conditioned by the use of exclusive language and by the identification of the male with the human discussed previously.

> If human beings are made in the Divine image but that image is male, then men and boys will be constantly re-enforced in their God-like identity and women will be considered and will consider themselves as other and less than human. (Smith, 1985, pp. 638-639)

Patriarchy also affects the materials used in church educational programs. Sexual discrimination exists in the pictures, stories, and curriculum in the Christian Church (Morton, 1985, p. 24).

> The church has published material that molds little children into these stereotyped roles while they are still in preschool. Before most children can utter the word God they have started to listen to culture tell them who they are. (Morton, 1985, p. 7)

If the Christian Gospel being proclaimed is truly inclusive, then the language used in proclaiming that Gospel needs to reflect the full range of inclusivity in the Church and especially with respect to the Divine. Since the language currently is not really inclusive, it follows that the Christian Gospel currently being proclaimed is not inclusive (Withers, 1984, pp. 11-12). "Resistance on the part of the church to deal with an inclusive gospel has made it clear that the theology we have known has been patriarchal to the core" (Morton, 1985, p. 20).

Inclusive Language within Christianity

The case for inclusive language in the Christian tradition has been made by, among others, Groome (1991), Hardesty (1987), Withers (1980 & 1984), and Wren (1989). Only one of the general approaches used in promoting inclusive language within Christianity is discussed here. This approach involves using the Christian Bible in various ways. One way is to point out the nature of Biblical translation. Another way uses Biblical verses to show how using only male language violates God's will as set forth in the Bible. A third way points to Jesus of Nazareth as portrayed in the Christian Scriptures. Each of these ways of using the Christian Bible is presented below.

Describing the ongoing nature of Biblical translation is one way to justify moving towards the use inclusive language in Christianity. The Bible is considered a sacred document by Christians, and the language used in the Bible to refer to the Divine has been and continues to be taken quite seriously. Much of the sexism in Christianity and the language used therein is based upon inaccurate or inappropriate translation of the Bible. With ongoing research, the accuracy of translations improves and a wider variety of names and images becomes available for use in the Christian Church (Throckmorton, 1985, pp. 527-528). In addition to the traditional masculine references to the Divine, such as "father" and "lord," the Bible also contains references like "mother," "midwife," "potter," "baker," "rock," and "light" (Groome, 1991, pp. 24-25). This variety of images in the Christian Bible supports the case for inclusive language, and using the full range of Biblical language referring to the Divine promotes inclusive language.

Using overwhelmingly male terms in referring to the Divine appears to be in conflict with two important Biblical injunctions. Using only or primarily male terms for the Divine may well lead to idolatry. Idolatry can be described as "the worship and/or perpetuation of any image or kind of image of God as though it were God" (Withers, 1984, p. 28). Idolatry stems from violating the Second Commandment, as found in Exodus 20:4: "You shall not make for yourself an idol, whether in the form of anything that is in heaven above, or that is on the earth beneath, or that is in the water under the earth" (NRSV). The traditional Christian practice of using an overwhelming amount of male terminology in referring to the Divine easily leads to identifying the male with the Divine when the Divine is claimed to be beyond both female and male. Such inappropriate identification may well be idolatrous. Using a variety of images could help prevent such inappropriate identification (Hardesty, 1987, p. 10).

Additionally, as Clarkson (1990, p. 44) suggests, using predominantly male-terms for the Divine and the so-called generics such as "man" and "he" violates the spirit of Galatians 3:28: "There is no longer Jew or Greek, there is no longer slave or free, there is no longer male and female, for all of you are one in Christ Jesus" (NRSV). Using a variety of images to refer to the Divine and a variety of ways to refer to human beings would appear to be more consistent with the claim made in Galatians 3:28 than are the current patriarchal practices.

In the portrayal of Jesus of Nazareth found in the Christian Bible, two points support the case for inclusive language. One point involves Jesus' attitude and behavior towards women. Wren (1989) suggests that the way Jesus behaved towards women was very extraordinary for his time and that this quite positive and non-patriarchal treatment of women may well have contributed to Jesus' death (Wren, 1989, pp. 175-182). Further, if Jesus is the model to imitate, then Christian men need to behave very differently. "Christian men are to give up male power and privilege and, by so doing, undermine the power and privilege of other patriarchal males" (Wren, 1989, p. 179). And part of the power and privilege of patriarchal males is control of the language. The second point involves noticing that Jesus' maleness is not important regarding salvation.

A son is male, and of course the historical person, Jesus, was a man. But as the Gospels depict Jesus, his maleness is not said to have any significance for salvation. It is the fact that Jesus was *human* that is crucial, both for Jesus' designation as the Christ and for Jesus' work of salvation. (Withers, 1986, p. 273)

First and foremost Jesus of Nazareth was a human being. "The Word became flesh" (John 1:14); this passage does not say that the word became male flesh.

Using inclusive language would help the Christian Church "recognize the inclusiveness of all humankind in the incarnation" (Withers, 1986, p. 12).

Inclusive Language as a Goal for Religious Education

That "the implementation of inclusive language is an important goal for religious education" (the third subthesis) is not directly supported by the explorations conducted in Chapters 3, 4, 5, and 6. The presentations in those chapters tend to be primarily descriptive, with only touches of the type of prescription needed to support this subthesis. These presentations indicate that if the views of Whitehead, Whorf, and Piaget are more accurate than not, then language is an important factor in thought, perception of reality, and behavior. In the following discussion, two general views of religious education are considered, one view of a traditional, conservative nature and the other of a more progressive nature. This discussion is intended to illustrate how the types of religious education and of theology adopted can influence the type of language used in the practice of that religious education and theology.

If religious education is viewed as communicating or training in a faith tradition, if that faith tradition and its theology are sexist, and if there is no movement for change within that tradition, then there would be neither the need nor the desire to implement inclusive language. In fact, one of the tasks of religious education in such a situation would be to perpetuate that tradition, including its sexism. Given the power of language, sexist language would be encouraged. Those religious groups that believe in and practice patriarchy, whether or not such belief and practice is openly admitted, will not want to use inclusive language, because such language would be potentially subversive. A Christian educator focused on conserving the tradition may want to reinforce "God the Father, Jesus the Son," for example.

Because society in the vast majority of its public outlets, such as the mass media, and Christianity in the vast majority of its traditional outlets are already patriarchal, not much effort is needed to perpetuate patriarchy. Nonetheless, a conserving educator may want to emphasize explicitly the traditional male-dominated nature of Christianity and may do so in lessons, prayers, conversation, pictures, and so on. Such an emphasis will provide much reinforcement for the students, developing those linguistic habits early, pouring foundation for later construction. Such a view of religious education would not support the claim that inclusive language is an important goal for religious education.

On the other hand, if religious education involves growing towards wholeness, justice, and fairness, then the case for inclusive language in religious education becomes stronger. For religious groups professing to promote inclusive, egalitarian forms of religion and who view religious education as one of the ways of moving closer towards such ideals, inclusive language can make a positive contribution. Some religious educators wish to be more inclusive in their language (and images) and to provide a more open, wide-ranging view of a Divine Parent, an eternal companion. Such a religious educator usually will have difficulty in getting immediately tangible results, given that the rest of the child's environmental influences (family, school, music, friends, and especially television) promote, however unconsciously and intentionally, sexist language and other patriarchal values. Perhaps the best a progressive religious educator can hope for is to plant some seeds in the patriarchal foundation of the child's experience, seeds that eventually may grow through the cracks in the foundation as they occur. If the child's family is on the same wavelength as the religious educator, then more hope is possible, though the outcome will still be in doubt due to the influence of the mass media and the other factors. Seeds may develop if and when the individual attains a critical consciousness regarding society, language, and patriarchy.

An inclusive type of religious education, as proposed in this study, is about the business of transforming individuals. Helping humans to treat each other with respect, care, and tolerance is part of this transforming process. Given the views of Whitehead, Whorf and Piaget, the language used throughout religious education, and especially throughout a child's environment, is important. The use of inclusive language is helpful in producing a more inclusive society by means of transforming persons and the religious communities in which those persons live. Therefore, "the implementation of inclusive language is an important goal for religious education."

Chapter 8
Implementing Inclusive Language

In the preceding chapters, the complex relationships between language, thought, perception and behavior as well as the stubbornness of sexist language and the possibilities for inclusive language have been explored using Whitehead's philosophy of organism, Whorf's linguistic relativity, and Piaget's genetic epistemology. Also, in the previous chapter, the importance of religious education was discussed. This study concludes with a more practical turn. In this chapter are found a presentation of some strategies for those individuals wishing to promote inclusive language in religious education; a discussion of some expectations and responses involved with implementing, or attempting to implement, inclusive language; and some concluding remarks.

Strategies

There are many ways to begin to implement inclusive language within religious education. In this section some general strategies that can contribute to the spread of inclusive language are considered. Before discussing the strategies themselves, some comments on the style or method of delivering an inclusive language strategy and on considering the audience when selecting a strategy are given.

How and when a strategy is used can be as important as the strategy itself; more generally, a strategy needs to be selected for the situation and the purpose of the educator. Some of these strategies are more appropriate for use with adults, especially the indirect techniques. Some of these strategies are more appropriate for use with children, such as flooding the environment with inclusive language and images. Some of these strategies can be used across age groups, as in the case of role-modeling. Further, an appropriate mixture of humor and seriousness, passion and lightness, lecturing and listening for a particular situation is not always easy to find. Inclusive language educators need to know their audience—to know if confrontational or if gentle techniques are more likely to be effective. Also, while sometimes logic can help effect change in human beings, most change in human life is not due to rational thought (Smith, 1985, p. 640).(1) The following strategies contain a mixture of rational and nonrational factors. Given the stubbornness of sexist language, inclusive language educators need to consider their audiences when deciding which strategies and techniques to use, when to use them, and how to use them.

---

1 Any logical approach can, and many times will, be rationalized. However, given the philosophy of organism, there can be long-term benefits to giving rational arguments which then become part of the process and can be pondered.

Role-modeling and Self-Critique

Persons who believe in and support inclusive language need to practice what they preach; that is, persons need to begin modeling in their own language, spoken and written, the type of language they wish others to use (Russell, 1985, p. 596). Role-modeling on the part of the educator is an appropriate strategy for all age groups. Otherwise, to claim to be inclusive and then to use language carelessly and in a sexist manner will leave one open to a charge of inconsistency. In order to model inclusive language, a person needs to be more self-conscious in language usage, to speak and write more slowly, with more thought and care.

> Self-conscious language use requires us to conscientiously examine virtually every word that comes to mind *before* we say it and confront the PUD (Patriarchal Universe of Discourse) conceptual structures we're striving to supplant and, simultaneously, create new ways of thinking. (Penelope, 1990, p. 213)

Advocates of inclusive language should critically examine their own language because old linguistic habits are plentiful, deeply buried, and hard to eliminate.

Penelope (1990), who directs her work towards women, makes a number of strategic suggestions that can be used by all those who wish to participate in the advance of inclusive language. These suggestions apply to individuals as well as to collectives. One suggestion is to identify and explain linguistic tricks as soon and as often as one notices them (Penelope, 1990, pp. 175-179). For example, the terms domestic violence and pedophilia mask the male agency that causes the vast majority of both kinds of violence (Penelope, 1990, pp. 209-211).

A second suggestion made by Penelope (1990) involves using humor to deflate patriarchal pretensions. "One way of developing our [women's] own place is to laugh at theirs [men's], to refuse to take their [men's] posturing and deceits seriously" (Penelope, 1990, p. 236). This can occur privately as well as publicly. One can chuckle to oneself or with one's friends at patriarchal language and habits. One also can use humor in front of the crowd, though some care may be needed since male reactions to public embarrassment can include physical violence or some other form of revenge. Nevertheless, humor appropriately used can be a powerful tool in the struggle for inclusive language.

Even more to the point, Penelope (1990) suggests that "the surest way to end our [women's] complicity in the construction of male discourse is to stop pretending we're dumb" (Penelope, 1990, p. 229). According to Penelope, women need to develop their own ways of describing their experience and to become active creators of language, that is, to become "conscious speakers of English" (Penelope, 1990, pp. 234 & 236).

More Strategies

Strategies for promoting inclusive language come in a variety of styles, ranging from more directly confrontational approaches to more subtle indirect approaches. An effective strategy for encouraging inclusive language in a given situation depends upon such factors as how well the educator knows the audience, the age of the audience, the expectations of the audience, the intent of the educator, the format of the presentation, the level of trust that exists between the educator and the audience, the length of the meeting time, and so on.

For example, an educator might want to shock an audience in order to stimulate thinking about sexist language issues and so might use techniques that directly confront patriarchal habits, such as referring to Goddess instead of God. Such a strategy runs the risk of creating too much dissonance (see Chapter 5 regarding Piaget), thereby causing most, if not all, of the audience to tune out the educator. On the other hand, the educator may choose to model inclusive language and not to raise the issue overtly. The danger in this approach is that the role-modeling will not disturb the equilibrium enough to stimulate learning (see Chapter 5 regarding Piaget). In both situations, however, inclusive language will have been introduced and become part of the past and therefore of the initial data for future events (see Chapter 3 regarding Whitehead).

In the following paragraphs four strategies are presented. These strategies may differ in style but the goal, the implementation of inclusive language, is the same. In light of contextual and developmental differences discussed in earlier chapters, multiple strategies are needed to encourage inclusive language.

One strategy, perhaps most appropriate with progressive adult audiences, in the promotion of inclusive language involves shattering the old, patriarchal images, especially of Divinity. The shattering of exclusive or limited images makes room available for more positive, inclusive images (Morton, 1985, pp. xxii, 151, & 195-196). Piagetian thought supports the belief that human beings acquire images very early in life and these images are very difficult to alter. While intellectual concepts can be altered, images must be shattered (Morton, 1985, p. 181). For example, one of these deeply ingrained images is that of "God the Father."

> But to substitute Goddess, an exclusively female image, and one classed as pagan, in the place of God immediately confronts the maleness in God, which produces a shock, a shattering, and opens the way for exorcising the old image. (Morton, 1985, p. 151)

Other techniques that directly confront patriarchal images include reversing labels in religious institutions as well as elsewhere. Reversing the labels would include using language that contradicts the image of God as a kindly, elderly man: for example, using Mother Goddess in lieu of Father God (Morton, 1985, pp. 6 & 195-196). By shattering the old images and metaphors, the growth and development of language is encouraged. "It is mainly through metaphor that language expands and is enriched; that new words emerge; that social, personal, and political changes are forged" (Morton, 1985, p. 172).

A second strategy, perhaps most appropriate with older children and young adults, involves getting the attention of the audience and "bending the tree the other way" (Smith, 1985b, p. 27). Getting the attention of the class or audience can be done in shocking ways or more subtle ways. One exercise that can be used to get the attention of persons involves a discussion of who changes their name at marriage; usually, young women tend to be more willing to alter their surnames, while young men tend to be adamant about not changing their surnames (Smith, 1985b, pp. 28-31). Another exercise suggests comparing the commonly described characteristics of a mature person, a mature man, and a mature woman (Smith, 1985b, pp. 28-21). Making such comparisons can easily lead to a discussion of societal stereotypes and the role of language in perpetuating those stereotypes.

"Bending the tree the other way" involves using feminine imagery and language in the place of patriarchal images and language. After thousands of years of patriarchal language, counterbalancing is needed (Smith, 1985b, p. 27). One suggestion encourages the use of only female references, including Goddess, for 30 days. Smith believes that those who participate in such an exercise "will never be the same" (Smith, 1985a, p. 641). Getting an audience's attention and then "bending the tree the other way" rarely occurs easily. Sometimes both processes can be encouraged at the same time. "We can always call beings *she* just to get people's attention and to force them to rethink their habitual choice of *he* and the expectations and assumptions about gender that underlie that choice" (Sheldon, 1990, p. 6).

A third strategy for implementing inclusive language tends to be more indirect than either of the preceding strategies. This approach involves the audience in various exercises that draw upon their own experiences as the basis for discussion. This strategy would seem most appropriate for adult audiences, although some of the techniques could be used with children and young adults. Discussion can include the following topics: comparing the participants' earliest understandings of the Divine (Withers, 1980, p. 9); the theology implicit in the various hymns and prayers used in worship (Withers, 1980, p. 9); the participants' experiences of being left out (or excluded) as well as their positive experiences of being included in a group (Withers, 1980, pp. 10-12); and the traits that the participants believe the Divine to possess, including the sources of those traits, the authority of those sources, and the adequacy of those traits to experience (Withers, 1980, pp. 7-8). In all cases the discussion initially focuses on issues other than language, and then is brought around to deal more directly with sexist and inclusive language issues.

Another indirect exercise involves having the participants imagine what kind of world they would like to live in if they did not know what skin color or ethnicity or sex they would be; Joanmarie Smith has wondered "what men might consider to be just if they had to fancy a world in which they did not know whether they were going to be women or men" (Smith, 1985a, p. 638). In this strategy, the subjects of sexist and inclusive language are not raised directly but are discussed as they occur in the discussion or when they are raised by the participants.

A fourth strategy, especially appropriate to young children, would be to flood their environment with inclusive language and images. This environment includes the family, the home, relatives, school, the mass media, the appropriate religious institution (mosque, temple, synagogue, church), and friends. A family using inclusive language faces a difficult task when the rest of the environment does not cooperate. Currently the rest of the environment does not cooperate very well. This strategy may be the most difficult to implement due to the multiplicity of persons, sub-environments, and other factors (such as moneymaking) involved. Also this strategy can easily expand into efforts to influence the language and images presented in non-home environments; for example, letters could be sent to television stations regarding their programming. This strategy has great long-term potential given the views of Whitehead, Whorf, and Piaget. The more inclusive language becomes part of the data, the more likely is the possibility of children growing up with inclusive thought, perception, and behavior.

Other suggestions, including specific techniques, are available, both for general use and for specifically Christian use. Some of the more general references include Maggio (1987), Nilsen et al. (1977), and Warren (1986). Some of the more specific Christian references include Hardesty (1987), Withers (1980), Withers (1984), and Groome (1991). With most of the suggestions, humor and patience are needed to help people to discuss the issues involved. Nevertheless, the basic goal is to increase awareness of the power of linguistic habits and to encourage the development of new linguistic habits.

> The way to escape from the distortions imposed by one's language is to acquire different conceptual systems that are presented by different languages. As you do this, you are actually using language to counteract the influences on our thinking of an unsophisticated use of language. (Lamb as cited in Regan, 1982, p. 29)

Responses

Lest anyone think that the implementation of inclusive language will be easy—it won't! Usually, inclusive language is neither easily implemented nor joyfully accepted. Sexist imagery and wording is buried deep in the human psyche and a few lexical changes will not have much impact (Morton, 1985, p. 194). The emotions associated with sexist imagery and wording are more ingrained than ideas about sexism: "[E]ducation for change involves first overcoming resistance to change. Attitudes are highly resistant to change" (Withers, 1984, p. 33). In fact, some individuals may never be able to change their sexist language, unless some form of shock learning works. For such people, the male-as-the-norm "is so unconscious and so taken-for-granted" that change is very difficult, if not nearly impossible. Ruether explains, "The invisibility of women can never be seen by those for whom the generic 'man' is simply assumed to include 'women'" (Ruether, 1985, p. 58). One should even expect that much of the maintenance of the status quo and the opposition to change will come from women.

> Not the least of our learnings is that the majority of women like the church and society the way they are. These 'Aunt Jane's' want to continue to be protected and supported. They want to be without sustained community and political responsibility. They like to be thought of, and treated as, the children they have become. (Morton, 1985, p. 5)

On this point, then, there is agreement: Expect Resistance!

Accordingly, the struggle for inclusive language, like other struggles for inclusiveness and human rights, will require time, patience, and persistence, as well as self-conscious and intentional activity towards the intended goal. There will be disappointments along the way; there will also be some successes. In changing, or trying to change, language, these words of advice are wise: "[C]aution: you are entering a solemn realm, an inner psychological world carefully built up and in balance" (Withers, 1984, p. 34). Since such change takes time, one needs patience, confidence in the belief that Goddess is working with you, and comfort in the knowledge that one is expected to be faithful, not always successful (Withers, 1984, p. 34).

For those who favor inclusive language and who begin the process of incorporating inclusive language into their own linguistic usage, a number of benefits may well follow. One consequence is that their awareness and understanding of inclusive language may begin to expand to include "our art and myths and gestures as well as our prosaic speech" (Moore, 1985, p. 614). This consequence is to be expected given the perspectives presented in this study; if language affects thought, perception, and behavior, then language also affects other forms of human expression, such as art and gesture. Another value occurs from the naming of Divinity as She and in using a variety of images in doing so, such as mother, sister, mid-wife. "Since that society downgrades and disvalues what it labels feminine,' naming God as She means facing that downgrading head-on and hoping to break through it" (Wren, 1989, pp. 161-162). Confronting, revealing, and dealing with biases in constructive ways is healthy. A third benefit, related to the second, is that expanding and enriching our vocabulary about the Divine will lead to an enrichment of devotional life and to an increased awareness of sensitivity and prejudice, thereby making us better neighbors (Hardesty, 1987, p. 14).

There are some negative possibilities associated with changing to inclusive language. One danger for those who really favor inclusive language is going too fast with the changes and scaring off individuals who are willing to change but who need to go more slowly in adapting to the changes and enjoying some of the benefits. A second adverse possibility involved with making changes too rapidly in a given situation is that a loss of financing as well as membership may ensue. Neither of these consequences need be a compelling reason for not going ahead with implementing inclusive language, but they are consequences that need to be considered in the move towards inclusive language.

One form of resistance to inclusive language comes in the guise of lukewarm support. Smith (1985b, pp. 28-31) points out that in many instances apparent support for inclusive language is really only a concession, perhaps given in order to avoid open argument and not because of any convictions on the matter. The sexist linguistic habits are given a temporary veneer that comes off easily when a change in the group occurs. Those without conviction on the matter grow tired, bored, and impatient with the issue of language and want to move on to some more important topic.

Eight objections to inclusive language regularly appear. In the following paragraphs each of these objections, as well as an appropriate response is presented.

The *denial* objection occurs when claims are made that language is neutral and that the real problem is in the sexist attitudes that lead to sexist language (Penelope, 1990, pp. 254-255; Wren, 1989, pp. 63-64). Sexist attitudes are important, and as the presentations on the perspectives of Whitehead, Whorf, and Piaget suggest, the relationship between attitudes and language is complex. Attitudes affect language, and language affects attitude. Also, if language were truly neutral, then using, for example, the generic "she" should be no problem, but since such usage is clearly a problem in the society of the U.S.A. today, the language is not neutral.

The *creativity* objection occurs when the claim is made that eliminating sexist expressions from English results in a stifling of the creativity of the writer (Penelope, 1990, pp. 254-255). In response to this objection, one can argue that because there are so many options in English from which to choose, creativity is actually encouraged by inclusive language. What is being challenged are the sexist linguistic habits which have been taken for granted; breaking those stifling habits is being promoted.

The *trivialization* objection occurs when the claim is made that the real issues are substantial issues like "equal pay for equal work," that inclusive language is a distraction raised by confused feminists (Penelope, 1990, pp. 254-255; Withers, 1985b, p. 645; Wren, 1989, pp. 63-64). As indicated by the results of this study, language is not a trivial factor in human thought, perception, and behavior. Also, if inclusive language were really a trivial issue, then there were not be much difficulty in changing from sexist language to inclusive language; however, since there is much difficulty in changing from sexist language to inclusive language, inclusive language is not a trivial issue.

The *aesthetic* objection occurs when the claim is made that even if there is sexist language, the inclusive alternatives are not aesthetic and therefore can be rejected on the grounds of taste (Penelope, 1990, pp. 254-255). Aesthetics are, in part, a matter of habit and of social convention. New habits can be developed, as this study has indicated with respect to language. Likewise social conventions, as well as individual preferences, change over time; humans can consciously and intentionally direct the changes. Humans can be creative in developing new aesthetics. Eventually, enough experience of inclusive liturgies, including inclusive language, will lead to overcoming the awkwardness (Hughes, 1985, p. 621).

The *negativity* objection occurs when the claim is made that sexist language grows out of sexist social structures; changing the social structures will result in inclusive language (Penelope, 1990, pp. 254-255). Based upon the results of this study, the relationship between social structures and language is not unilateral. Social structures contribute to the perpetuation of sexism, and sexist language contributes to the continuation of sexist social structures. Implementing inclusive language would remove one of the supports for patriarchal social structures.

The *censorship* objection occurs when the claim is made that an author has the right to use English in whatever way the author wants, including sexist usages; to require inclusive language, it is claimed, constitutes a form of censorship (Penelope, 1990, pp. 254-255). By the same token, in the United States, publishing businesses do not have to accept writing that does not meet their stated criteria. Businesses with stated criteria that include the use of inclusive language need not accept sexist writing. Likewise, readers do not have to read material that does not meet their personal criteria; disapproval can be expressed by a refusal to purchase sexist writing. All of this has to do with "free market capitalism."

The *tradition* objection occurs when the claim is made that inclusive language is not traditional and therefore should not be implemented (Withers, 1985b, p. 645). But traditional views change over time. What was considered right and proper at one time, such as slavery, often comes to be viewed as wrong and improper at a later time. Tradition is a guide to be evaluated and followed if appropriate, not a legal or divine code to be rigidly observed.

The *sexist* objection occurs when a person uses sexist language and, when questioned on that usage, claims "I meant it and still do" (Wren, 1989, p. 64). This objection at least has the virtue of honesty. However, underneath this objection may be a well-founded fear—of losing one's security, of losing one's power, of being left behind. The process of language change can be frightening (Moore, 1985, p. 612). No logical response can be given to the sexist objection, but experiences can be created and undergone which could demonstrate that the fear may not be as serious as first felt or believed.

For many people, learning to use inclusive language will be like trying to break a long-standing habit. And breaking such a habit can be quite difficult, given the power of the past. The use of sexist language is such a habit, and while sexist language may not be as obviously destructive as some other habits, there remains the damage done by the long-standing habit, at both individual and societal levels. Further, breaking such a habit tends to be painful for all concerned, and developing a new habit is not always the best approach to take. However, unlike sexist linguistic habits which close off alternatives, inclusive linguistic habits open up more possibilities, a potentially ever-expanding critical consciousness.

> Language, like tobacco, is habit forming. Some patterns of writing and speaking are addictive and may damage both the user and others who breathe the same linguistic atmosphere. If we see the damage being done and decide to kick the habit, we may get withdrawal symptoms and hostility or derision from other smokers. But in the end, we shall enjoy breathing fresh air. (Wren, 1989, p. 83)

Moving toward more inclusive language, and thereby towards more inclusive societies, contributes to the health and strength of free individuals. Without such movement, society will continue to deteriorate. With such movement the chances for survival are increased.

> The art of free society consists first in the maintenance of the symbolic code; and secondly in fearlessness of revision, to secure that the code serves those purposes which satisfy an enlightened reason. Those societies which cannot combine reverence to their symbols with freedom of revision must ultimately decay either from anarchy or from the slow atrophy of a life stifled by useless shadows (Whitehead, 1959, p. 88).

Concluding Remarks

When working in the child care field, as I did for a number of years, one of my primary goals, inspired then by my readings of Whitehead and Piaget, was to help incorporate positive experiences into the specific life experiences of the children. One of the means of achieving this goal was role-modeling appropriate behavior, including using inclusive language as much as I knew at the time, mediating disputes in nonviolent ways, having fun, and so on. My belief then was that if positive experiences could be *put into the child's memory banks*, so to speak, then the child would always have some positive experiences to draw upon, perhaps unconsciously, and, in later life, those experiences, some of them even conscious, might help provide the growing child a foundation for better living.

Continued study of Whitehead's philosophy of organism and Piaget's genetic epistemology combined with explorations into Whorf's principle of linguistic relativity have deepened the beliefs held during my child care experiences. I have become even more aware of the various ways by which language often contributes to the continuation of patriarchy. Current linguistic practices tend to contribute not only to sexism, but also to racism, ethnocentrism, classism, and anthropocentrism. Developing inclusive linguistic habits in young children can help reduce societal support for patriarchy in all of its various forms.

If those who are more able to do so make conscious decisions and begin using inclusive language, then the inclusive data available in persons' experience will increase. Using inclusive language also will increase the inclusiveness of thought, perception, and behavior. Sexist linguistic habits that have developed can be altered, though such alteration will take time and effort, given the current dominance of sexist language. Planting inclusive language, non-patriarchal seeds, is possible; this can influence linguistic habits in such a way that the linguistic support for patriarchy will begin to erode.

From the perspectives of Whitehead, Whorf, and Piaget, this dissertation has become part of the past, part of the Divine's ever-adjusting vision for this cosmic epoch; it is already part of the process of working towards inclusive language. Language is part of the lens through which individuals understands reality, and changing language is necessary if individuals are to change perceptions of reality (Gray, 1982, pp. 36-46). Implementing truly inclusive language in religious education would help to usher in the day when

> A class of elementary school children were asked what they would like to be when they grow up. The girls named vocations such as doctor, lawyer, paleontologist, politician, nurse, and homemaker. The boys named vocations such as doctor, lawyer, paleontologist, politician, nurse, and homemaker. The children were then asked to pretend to be the opposite sex, and each child was asked again what they would like to be when they grow up. The girls named vocations such as doctor, lawyer, paleontologist, politician, nurse, and homemaker. The boys named vocations such as doctor, lawyer, paleontologist, politician, nurse, and homemaker.

And no boy would rather be dead than be a girl.

Bibliography

Anthony, E.J. (1976). Piaget's affective system: An appraisal. In J.D. Andrews (Ed.), *Early childhood education: It's an art? it's a science* (pp. 41-56). Washington, DC: National Association for the Education of Young Children.

Black, M. (1959). Linguistic relativity: The views of Benjamin Lee Whorf. *Philosophical Review*, 68, 228-238.

Bloom, A.H. (1981). *The linguistic shaping of thought: A study in the impact of language on thinking in China and the West*. Hillsdale, NJ: Erlbaum.

Boys, M.C. (1985). Language and the Bible: A response. *Religious Education*, 80(4), 539-549.

Brock, R.N. (1988). *Journeys by heart: A christology of erotic power*. New York, NY: Crossroad.

Butt, D. (1989). *Talking and thinking: The patterns of behavior* (2nd ed.). Oxford: Oxford University Press.

Carroll, J.B. (1953). *The study of language: A survey of linguistics and related disciplines in America*. Cambridge: Harvard University Press.

Carroll, L. (1992). Humpty dumpty. In G.L. Bowie, M.W. Michaels, & R.C. Solomon, (Eds.), *Twenty questions: An introduction to philosophy* (pp. 295-299). San Diego, CA: Harcourt Brace Jovanovich.

Clarkson, J.S. (1990). Inclusive language and the church. *Prism*, 5(2), 37-49.

Donaldson, M. (1978). *Children's minds*. New York: Norton.

Dreyer, P.F. (1984, Fall). Class notes from *Education 330: Cognitive development and education*. The Claremont Graduate School, Claremont, CA.

Durka, G., & Smith, J. (1976a). Modeling in religious education. *Religious Education*, 71(2), 115-132.

Durka, G., & Smith, J. (1976b). *Modeling God: Religious education for tomorrow*. New York: Paulist Press.

Faludi, S. (1991). *Backlash: The undeclared war against American women*. New York: Crown.

Fetz, V.R.L. (1988). On the formation of ontological concepts: The relationship between the theories of Whitehead and Piaget (C.W. Spanier & J.M. Sweeney, Trans.). *Process Studies*, 17(4), 262-272.

Feuer, L.S. (1953). Sociological aspects of the relation between language and philosophy. *Philosophy of   Science*, 20(2), 85-100.

Fishman, J.A. (1960). A systematization of the Whorfian hypothesis. *Behavioral Science*, 5, 323-339.

Fishman, J.A. (1980). The Whorfian hypothesis: Varieties of valuation, confirmation and disconfirmation: I. *International Journal of the Sociology of Language*, 26, 25-40.

Fishman, J.A. (1982). Whorfianism of the third kind: Ethnolinguistic diversity as a worldwide societal asset (the Whorfian hypothesis: Varieties of validation, confirmation, and disconfirmation II. *Language in Society*, 11(1), 1-14.

Flavell, J.H. (1963). *The developmental psychology of Jean Piaget*. Princeton: Van Nostrand.

Flavell, J.H. (1977). *Cognitive development*. Englewood Cliffs, NJ: Prentice Hall.

Frank, F.W., & Treichler, P.A. (1989). *Language, gender, and professional writing: Theoretical approaches and guidelines for nonsexist usage*. New York: Commission on the Status of Women in the Profession, Modern Language Association of America.

Franklin, S.T. (1990). *Speaking from the depths: Alfred North Whitehead's hermeneutical metaphysics of propositions, experience, symbolism, language, and religion*. Grand Rapids: Eerdmans.

Giltner, F.M. (Ed.). (1985). *Women's issues in religious education*. Birmingham: Religious Education   Press.

Ginsburg, H., & Opper, S. (1979). *Piaget's theory of intellectual development*. Englewood Cliffs, NJ: Prentice Hall.

Grant, J. (1989). *White women's Christ and black women's Jesus: Feminist christology and womanist   response*. Atlanta: Scholars Press.

Gray, E.D. (1981). *Green paradise lost*. Wellesley, MA: Roundtable Press.

Gray, E.D. (1982). *Patriarchy as a conceptual trap*. Wellesley, MA: Roundtable Press.

Griffin, D.R. (1992). [Review of *Speaking from the depths*]. *Journal of Religion*, 72(1), 124.

Groome, T.H. (1991). *Language for a 'Catholic' church*. Kansas City: Sheed & Ward.

Hardesty, N.A. (1987). *Inclusive language in the church*. Atlanta: John Knox.

Harris, M. (1988). *Women and teaching: Themes for a spirituality of pedagogy*. New York: Paulist Press.

Hendley, B. (1986). Alfred North Whitehead and the rhythm of education. Chap. 4 of *Dewey, Russell, Whitehead: Philosophers as educators*. Carbondale, IL: Southern Illinois University Press.

Holdcroft, D. (1991). *Saussure: Signs, system, and arbitrariness*. New York, NY: Cambridge University Press.

Holy Bible, new revised standard version. (1989).

Hughes, R.D., III. (1985). The case for inclusive language by a white male. *Religious Education*, 80(4), 616-633.

Jordan, D.C. (1974). The Anisa Model: A master plan for equalizing educational opportunity. *Meforum*, 1(3), 57-62.

Jordan, D.C. (1976). Early childhood education: It's a science. In J.D. Andrews (Ed.), *Early childhood education: It's an art? it's a science* (pp. 167-180). Washington, DC: National Association for the Education of Young Children.

Jordan, D.C. (1979). Rx for Piaget's complaint: A science of education. *Journal of Teacher Education*, 30(5), pp. 11-14.

Jordan, D.C., & Shepard, R.P. (1972). The philosophy of the Anisa Model. *World Order*, 7(1), 23-31.

Jordan, D.C., & Streets, D.T. (1973). The Anisa Model: A new basis for educational planning. *Young Children*, 28(5), 289-307.

Kalinowski, M.F., & Jordan, D.C. (1973). Being and becoming: The Anisa theory of development. *World Order*, 7(4), 17-26.

Kay, P., & Kempton, W. (1984). What is the Sapir-Whorf hypothesis. *American Anthropology*, 86(1), 65-79.

Kilbourne, J. (Narrator). (1987). *Still killing us softly* [Film], (M. Lazarus, Producer and Director). Cambridge: Cambridge Documentary Film.

Lakoff, G. (1987). *Women, fire, and dangerous things: What categories reveal about the mind*. Chicago: University of Chicago Press.

Lenneberg, E.H. (1967). *Biological foundations of language*. New York: Wiley.

Maggio, R. (1987). *The nonsexist word finder: A dictionary of gender-free usage*. Phoenix: Oryx.

Mays, W. (1972). Jean Piaget. In Paul Edwards (Ed.), *The encyclopedia of philosophy: Vol. 6*. New York: Macmillan & Free Press.

McCrum, R., Cran, W., & MacNeil, R. (1986). *The story of English*. New York: Sifton, Penguin.

Miller, R.C. (1985). Inclusive language: A response. *Religious Education*, 80(4), 571-581.

Miller, R.L. (1968). *The linguistic relativity principle and Humboldtian ethnolinguistics: A history and appraisal*. Hague: Mouton.

Moore, M.E. (1985). Inclusive language and power: A response. *Religious Education*, 80(4), 603-614.

Morton, N. (1985). *The journey is home*. Boston: Beacon.

Muhlhausler, P. & Harre, R. (1990). *Pronouns and people: The linguistic construction of social and   personal identity*. Oxford: Blackwell.

National Public Radio. (1992, September 7). Morning Edition. San Diego, CA: KPBS Radio. (8:08 A.M.)

Nilsen, A.P., Bosmajin, H., Gershung, H.L., & Stanley, J.P. (1977). *Sexism and language*. Urbana, IL: National Council of Teachers of English.

Olewiler, B.J. (1971). *Whitehead's philosophy of language and the Whorfian hypothesis*. Unpublished doctoral dissertation., John Hopkins University, Baltimore.

Penelope, J. (1990). *Speaking freely: Unlearning the lies of the fathers' tongue*. Elmsford, NY: Pergamon.

Penn, J.M. (1972). *Linguistic relativity versus innate ideas: The origins of the Sapir-Whorf hypothesis in   German thought*. Hague: Mouton.

Phillips, J.L., Jr. (1969). *The origins of intellect: Piaget's theory*. San Francisco: Freeman.

Piaget, J. (1952). *The origins of intelligence in children* (2nd ed.) (M. Cook, Trans.). New York: International Universities Press.

Piaget, J. (1962). *Comments on Vygotsky's critical remarks* (A. Parsons, Trans.), (E. Haufmann & G. Vakar, Eds.). Cambridge: MIT Press.

Piaget,J. (1970). *Genetic epistemology* (E. Duckworth, Trans.). NewYork: Norton.

Piaget, J. (1971a). *Biology and knowledge: An essay on the relations between organic regulations and cognitive processes* (B. Walsh, Trans.). Chicago: University of Chicago Press. (Original work published 1967)

Piaget, J. (1971b). *Insights and illusions of philosophy* (W. Mays, Trans.). New York: World. (Original work published 1965)

Piaget, J. (1971c). *Psychology and epistemology* (A. Rosin, Trans.). New York: Viking. (Original work published 1970)

Piaget, J. (1972). Intellectual evolution from adolescence to adulthood (J. Bliss & H. Furth, Trans.). *Human Development*, 15(1), 1-12. (Original work published 1970)

Piaget, J. (1973). *To understand is to invent* (G. Roberts, Trans.). New York, NY: Grossman Publishers, The Viking Press. (Original work published 1948)

Piaget, J. (1974). *The language and thought of the child* (2nd ed.), (M. & R. Gabain, Trans.). New York: Meridian, New American Library. (Original 2nd edition published 1930)

Piaget J. (Narrator). (1977). *Piaget on Piaget: The epistemology Jean Piaget* [Videorecording], (C. Goretta, Dir.). New Haven: Media Design Studio, Yale University.

Piaget, J. & Inhelder, B. (1969). *The psychology of the child* (H. Weaver, Trans.). New York: Basic. (Original work published 1966)

Piattelli-Palmarini, M. (Ed.). (1980). *Language and learning: The debate between Jean Piaget and Noam Chomsky*. Cambridge: Harvard University Press.

Pinxten, R. (Ed.). (1976). *Universalism versus relativism in language and thought: Proceedings of a colloquium on the Sapir-Whorf hypotheses*. Hague: Mouton.

Poynton, C. (1989). *Language and gender: Making the difference* (2nd ed.). New York: Oxford University Press.

Raman, S.P. (1975). Role of nutrition in the actualization of the potentialities of the child: An Anisa perspective. *Young Children*, 31(1), 24-32.

Regan, J.O. (Ed.). (1982). *Whitehead and Lamb: A new network of connection*. Claremont, CA: The Claremont Graduate School. [Second in a series of seminars on Issues in Communication].

Regan, J.O. (Ed.). (1988a). *Semiotics in education: A dialogue*. Claremont, CA: The Claremont Graduate School. [Tenth in a series of seminars on Issues in Communication].

Regan, J.O. (Ed.). (1988b). *Using language and knowing how*. Claremont, CA: The Claremont Graduate School. [Twelfth in a series of seminars on Issues in Communication].

Regan, J.O. (Ed.). (1989). *The eye of the dragon*. Claremont, CA: The Claremont Graduate School. [Thirteenth in a series of seminars on Issues in Communication].

Reuther, R. (1985, March 4). How not to reinvent the wheel: Feminist theology in the academy. *Christianity and Crisis*, 45(3), 57-62.

Rollins, P.C. (1980). *Benjamin Lee Whorf: Lost generation theories of mind, language, and religion*. Ann Arbor: Publ. for Popular Culture Association by University Microfilms International.

Rothwell, J.D. (1982). *Telling it like it isn't: Language misuse & malpractice; what we can do about it*. Englewood Cliffs, NJ: Prentice Hall.

Russell, L.M. (1974). *Human liberation in a feminist perspective: A theology*. Philadelphia: Westminster.

Russell, L.M. (Ed.). (1976). *The liberating word: A guide to nonsexist interpretation of the Bible*. Philadelphia: Westminster.

Russell, L.M. (1985). Inclusive language and power. *Religious Education*, 80(4), 582-602.

Russell, L.M. (1987). *Household of freedom: Authority in feminist theology*. Philadelphia: Westminster Press.

Russell, L.M., Pui-lan, K., Isasi-Diaz, A.M., & Cannon, K.G. (Eds.). (1988). *Inheriting our mothers' gardens: Feminist theology in third world perspective*. Philadelphia: Westminister.

Salmon, M. (1990). The function of canon and the quest for inclusive language. *Prism*, 5(2), 50-56.

Sanborn, D.A. (1971). *The language process: Toward a holistic schema with implications*. Hague: Mouton.

Sapir, E. (1949). *Language: An introduction to the study of speech*. New York: Harvest; Harcourt, Brace, & World.

Schultz, E.A. (1990). *Dialogues at the margins: Whorf, Bakhtin, and linguistic relativity*. Madison: University of Wisconsin Press.

Seymour, J.L., & Miller, D.E. (1982). *Contemporary approaches to Christian education*. Nashville: Abingdon.

Sheldon, A. (1990). Kings are royaler than queens: Language and socialization. *Young Children*, 45(2), 4-9.

Smith, J. (1985a). Case for inclusive language: A response. *Religious Education*, 80(4), 634-643.

Smith, J. (1985b). Language again and still. In F.M. Giltner (Ed.), *Women's Issues in Religious Education* (pp. 27-40). Birmingham: Religious Education Press.

Streets, D.T. (1976). Preschool and early math instruction: A developmental approach. In J.D. Andrews (Ed.), *Early childhood education: It's an art? it's a science* (pp. 75-90). Washington, D. C.: National Association for the Education of Young Children.

Streets, D.T., & Jordan, D.C. (1973). Guiding the process of becoming: The Anisa theories of curriculum and teaching. *World Order*, 7(4), 29-40.

Thistlethwaite, S.B. (1985). Inclusive language: Theological and philosophical fragments. *Religious Education*, 80(4), 551-570.

Throckmorton, B.H., Jr. (1985). Language and the Bible. *Religious Education*, 80(4), 523-538.

Trager, G.L. (1959). The systematization of the Whorf hypothesis. *Anthropological Linguistics*, 1(1), 31-35.

Wallace, M. (Producer). (1985). *Baby talk* [Television transcript]. Boston: WGBH Educational Foundation.

Warren, V.L. (1986). Guidelines for nonsexist use of language [abridged version]. Originally published in *Proceedings and Addresses of the American Philosophical Association*, 59(3), 471-482.

Weis, L. (Ed.). (1988). *Class, race, and gender in American education.* Albany: State University of New York Press.

Westerhoff, J.H., III. (Ed.). (1985). Inclusive language. *Religious Education,* 80(4).

Whitehead, A.N. (1948). *Science and philosophy.* New York: Wisdom, Philosophical Library.

Whitehead, A.N. (1958). *The function of reason.* Boston: Beacon. (Original work published 1929)

Whitehead, A.N. (1959). *Symbolism: Its meaning and effect.* New York: Capricorn, Putnam. (Original work published 1927)

Whitehead, A.N. (1961a). *Adventures of ideas.* New York: Free Press. (Original work published 1933)

Whitehead, A.N. (1961b). *The interpretation of science: Selected essays* (A.H. Johnson, Ed.). New York: Bobbs Merrill.

Whitehead, A.N. (1966). *Modes of thought.* New York: Free Press. (Original work published 1938)

Whitehead, A.N. (1967a). *The aims of education and other essays.* New York: Free Press. (Original work published 1929)

Whitehead, A.N. (1967b). *Science and the modern world.* New York: Free Press. (Original work published 1925)

Whitehead, A.N. (1974). *Religion in the making.* New York: Meridian, New American Library. (Original work published 1926)

Whitehead, A.N. (1978). *Process and reality: An essay in cosmology* (corrected ed.), (D.R. Griffin & D.W. Sherburne, Eds.). New York: Free Press. (Original work published 1929).

Whorf, B.L. (1956). *Language, thought, and reality: Selected writings of Benjamin Lee Whorf* (J.B. Carroll, Ed.). Cambridge: MIT Press.

Williams, D.S. (1985). Women's oppression and lifeline politics in black women's religious narratives. *Journal of Feminist Studies in Religion,* 1(2), 59-71.

Williams, D.S. (1986). The color of feminism: Or speaking the black woman's tongue. *Journal of Religious Thought,* 43(1), 42-58.

Withers, B.A. (Ed.). (1980). *Language about god in liturgy and scripture: A study guide*. Philadelphia: Publ. for Joint Educational Development by Geneva Press.

Withers, B.A. (Ed.). (1984). *Language and the church: Articles and designs for workshops*. New York: Division of Publication Services, National Council of the Churches of Christ in the U.S.A.

Withers, B.A. (1985a). Inclusive language and religious education. *Religious Education*, 80(4), 507-521.

Withers, B.A. (1985b). Suggestions for study. *Religious Education*, 80(4), 644-653.

Withers, B.A. (Ed.). (1986). *An inclusive-language lectionary: Readings for year A, revised edition*. Atlanta: John Knox.

Wren, B. (1989). *What language shall I borrow? God-talk in worship: A male response to feminist theology*. New York: Crossroad.

About the Author

John Sweeney is a Cubs fan . . . which means that he knows more about hope than the average person.

At an earlier time in his life John was a collector of academic degrees and, during that long season, earned a B.A. from Illinois College, an M.Div. from Union Theological Seminary in New York City, an M.A. in Philosophy from University of Nebraska-Lincoln, and a Ph.D. from Claremont School of Theology. This current book is a revised version of his doctoral dissertation.

Dr. Sweeney currently is Managing Director of the Center for Process Studies in Claremont, CA; he also serves as Adjunct Instructor in Theology for the Claremont School of Theology, where he delights in introducing students to Process Thought. Prior to his Claremont season, John taught introductory philosophy and religion courses for ten years in the California Community College system.

A lifelong (and active) member of the United Church of Christ, John is married to UCC minister, Rev. Dr. Sharon Graff. They happily live with two cats in a geodesic domehome in the middle of the forest in Southern California.

For more conversation about "life, the universe, and everything" John may be reached at sweeney@ctr4process.org.